The
Next Phase
of Total
Quality
Management

QUALITY AND RELIABILITY

A Series Edited by

EDWARD G. SCHILLING
Coordinating Editor
Center for Quality and Applied Statistics
Rochester Institute of Technology
Rochester, New York

W. GROVER BARNARD
Associate Editor for
Human Factors
Vita Mix Corporation
Cleveland, Ohio

RICHARD S. BINGHAM, JR.
Associate Editor for
Quality Management
Consultant
Brooksville, Florida

LARRY RABINOWITZ
Associate Editor for
Statistical Methods
College of William and Mary
Williamsburg, Virginia

THOMAS WITT
Associate Editor for
Statistical Quality Control
Rochester Institute of Technology
Rochester, New York

ADDITIONAL VOLUMES IN PREPARATION

The Next Phase of Total Quality Management

TQM II and the Focus on Profitability

Robert E. Stein

Robert Stein Consulting
Cedar Park, Texas

Marcel Dekker, Inc.   **New York • Basel • Hong Kong**

Library of Congress Cataloging-in-Publication Data

Stein, Robert E.
    The next phase of total quality management : TQM II and the focus
on profitability / Robert E. Stein.
      p.   cm. — (Quality and reliability ; 42)
    Includes bibliographical reference and index.
    ISBN 0-8247-9110-X
    1. Total quality management. I. Title. II. Series.
HD62.15.S76   1993   93-5802
658.5'62-dc20   CIP

The publisher offers discounts on this book when ordered in bulk quantities. For
more information, write to Special Sales/Professional Marketing at the address below.

This book is printed on acid-free paper.

Marcel Dekker, Inc.
270 Madison Avenue, New York, New York 10016

Current printing (last digit):
10 9 8 7 6 5 4 3 2 1

PRINTED IN THE UNITED STATES OF AMERICA

To my wife, Debera, for her love and support,
and to my daughters, Jennifer and Allyson.

About the Series

The genesis of modern methods of quality and reliability will be found in a simple memo dated May 16, 1924, in which Walter A. Shewhart proposed the control chart for the analysis of inspection data. This led to a broadening of the concept of inspection from emphasis on detection and correction of defective material to control of quality through analysis and prevention of quality problems. Subsequent concern for product performance in the hands of the user stimulated development of the systems and techniques of reliability. Emphasis on the consumer as the ultimate judge of quality serves as the catalyst to bring about the integration of the methodology of quality with that of reliability. Thus, the innovations that came out of the control chart spawned a philosophy of control of quality and reliability that has come to include not only the methodology of the statistical sciences and engineering, but also the use of appropriate management methods together with various motivational procedures in a concerted effort dedicated to quality improvement.

This series is intended to provide a vehicle to foster interaction of the elements of the modern approach to quality, including statistical applications, quality and reliability engineering, management, and motivational aspects. It is a forum in which the subject matter of these various areas can be brought together to allow for effective integration of appropriate techniques. This will promote the true benefit of each, which can be achieved only through their interaction. In this sense, the whole of quality and reliability is greater than the sum of its parts, as each element augments the others.

The contributors to this series have been encouraged to discuss fundamental concepts as well as methodology, technology, and procedures at the leading edge of the discipline. Thus, new concepts are placed in proper perspective in these evolving disciplines. The series is intended for those in manufacturing, engineering, and marketing and management, as well as the consuming public, all of whom have an interest and stake in the improvement and maintenance of quality and reliability in the products and services that are the lifeblood of the economic system.

The modern approach to quality and reliability concerns excellence: excellence when the product is designed, excellence when the product is made, excellence as the product is used, and excellence throughout its lifetime. But excellence does not result without effort, and products and services of superior quality and reliability require an appropriate combination of statistical, engineering, management, and motivational effort. Furthermore, excellence does not guarantee the success of any company in achieving the goal of increased profitability. It should be realized that the knowledge and techniques needed to accomplish this task may be somewhat broader than originally conceived. This effort can be directed for maximum benefit only in light of timely knowledge of approaches and methods that have been developed and are available in these areas of expertise. Within the volumes of this series, the reader will find the means to create, control, correct, and improve quality and reliability in ways that are cost effective from a global perspective, that enhance productivity, and that create a motivational atmosphere that is harmonious and constructive. It is dedicated to that end and to the readers whose study of quality and reliability will lead to greater understanding of their products, their processes, their workplaces, and themselves.

Edward G. Schilling

Preface

In recent years, articles have begun to appear in major publications which address the failure of Total Quality Management (TQM) in America. *Newsweek*'s September 7, 1992, article states, "The Cost of Quality: Faced with Hard Times, Business Sours on Total Quality Management." The article goes on to present many different views from various companies about their experiences with TQM. While some have been successful, others have failed miserably. A 1992 Rath and Strong survey was quoted as grading companies on TQM efforts for "improving market share," "reining in costs" and "making customers happy." It seems that most companies rated Ds and Fs. Only 36% of the companies surveyed by Arthur D. Little said that TQM was having "a significant impact" on their ability to compete. The article goes on to state the U.S. companies have "soured" because they find "little protection against hard time." Is this technology so difficult that most companies either are unwilling to stay with it long enough or find that their people are unable to implement it?

While various reasons have been given for this failure, the supposed cause has usually been attributed to a failure of management to implement TQM properly. The solution offered by the experts has usually been to try harder. However, many questions have begun to be raised as to whether the current brand of TQM is at issue and not the level of implementation achieved. Chapter 1 presents the results of a Governmental Accounting Office study of the twenty top-scoring Malcolm Baldrige Award applicants from 1988 and 1989. The impact on profitability for corporations which supposedly implemented TQM better than any other companies in the country has not met expectations.

Whether anyone wants to admit it the objective of TQM is to address the profitability issue. If it does not, then it must be considered a solution for which a problem must now be found. So what is the difference between those companies who have succeeded in increasing profits and those who have failed? Those companies that have succeeded in increasing profits did so by solving problems that related directly to profitability. By understanding more about the relationship between the corporate environment and profitability, an improved mechanism can be developed that will accelerate the rate at which companies succeed.

The objective in writing this book is to create an improved platform within the TQM umbrella for supporting the profit motive. This book presents and expands the body of knowledge within the Theory of Constraints pioneered by Dr. Eliyahu M. Goldratt. It includes an augmentation of the Total Quality Management methodology and presents a process of "continuous profit improvement" sorely needed for today's hard-pressed manufacturing companies. It presents new tools for managing and focusing change dedicated to increasing profitability and addresses the implementation of the traditional tools from a global perspective in supporting the profitability issues.

• • •

These concepts have been proven to accelerate dramatically the profitability of *any* company.

• • •

To provide a proper foundation, the initial thrust of the book is devoted to changing the paradigms associated with traditional management strategies and then offering a logical solution as well as a platform upon which to build the new structure. It provides guidelines for implementation as well as insights into the strategic issues.

Chapters 1 through 6 represent a logical progression from the creation of absolute measurements used to guide the "continuous profit improvement" process to the creation of an enhanced method of shop floor management. It addresses the impact of establishing valid policy systems and offers an improved method for addressing the physical environment.

Once the basis for change has been developed, Chapters 7 and 8 provide a platform for implementation, defining TQM II and outlining organizational and communications strategies. It is one thing to say something must be done. It is another to provide a global picture and to say who is responsible and how it can be accomplished.

Chapters 9 through 12 discuss well-established traditional tools such as Quality Function Deployment (QFD), Design for Manufacturability, Statistical Process Control (SPC) and Design of Experiments (DOE) from a traditional as well as global perspective, indicating what must be done to modify each to take advantage of those discoveries made thus far.

Chapters 13 and 14 discuss concepts of implementation and strategy. Once the reader is armed with full knowledge of what must be done, how to accomplish as well as fine-tune the overall strategy must be addressed.

The benefits of understanding the concepts behind the creation of TQM II and a successful implementation will prove invaluable. In the past five years many companies have found refuge in the implementation of the technology discussed in this text. How much change in profitability has been experienced varies from company to company, as would be expected. However, those changes which have been documented range anywhere from 70% in one year to 600% in six months. How quickly they occur and whether improvements continue is in direct relation to where the company is prior to starting the implementation and the company's ability to consistently implement the concepts discussed in this text. It really does not matter what the industry is.

Special thanks to the following people for helping to make this book possible: Cy Daws for his guidance, persistence and encouragement and Len Doty for his contributions and help in organizing Chapter 7.

Robert E. Stein

Contents

1

Introducing the TQM II Concept

• • •

For us to merely duplicate the efforts of our most worthy opponent is to condemn ourselves to mediocrity. It is time we recognized that we can improve on the current level of understanding.

• • •

This chapter gives a brief definition of traditional Total Quality Management (TQM), introduces the TQM II concept and lays the groundwork for what is to follow in later chapters.

OBJECTIVES

- To introduce the concept of TQM II.
- To provide an overview for the text.

TOTAL QUALITY MANAGEMENT DEFINED

Traditional Total Quality Management (TQM) offers a management philosophy and structure designed to improve the profitability of companies through the practice of continuously improving all facets of each functional area including the management process. The TQM umbrella includes the application of statistical methodologies which support a process of constantly monitoring the degree of variability within processes and for determining cause and effect relationships. Employee involvement as well as cross-functional management teams are used to manage the implementation of the improvement process and to focus on areas within the company which need improvement. Focusing mechanisms are designed to continuously improve the quality of products and activities while reducing costs.

Establishing the Need for Change

American businesses must never lose sight of the fact that the "goal" of any business is to create wealth. But how do current day TQM/TQC programs focus on this issue? Good quality is a requirement placed on each company by its customers. Unless a company is perceived by the customer as providing good quality at an acceptable price the customer will probably not spend money for the company's products or services. But, fulfilling the requirement of good quality does not guarantee that the company will sell more product.

In order to create an improvement in profitability, "sales" must move up while Inventory and Operating Expense move down. However, once success has been gained in fulfilling the requirement of good quality, even when quality is defined in its broadest terms, any further increase in quality may only increase the *potential* for increasing sales and not the sales figure itself. How then must the requirement of good quality be satisfied while achieving the goal of increased profits? What actions must be taken to link the process of improvement to profitability?

Whenever discussions of the success or failure of any project within the company are entertained they must be judged based on their impact on profitability. Figure 1.1 is a compilation of the results of a May 1991 government study on 20 of the highest scoring Malcolm Baldrige Award applicants from 1988 and 1989. The results are very interesting.

Performance Indicator	Average Annual Improvement
Employee Satisfaction	1.4%
Reliability	11.3%
Reduction in Processing Time	12.0%
Reduction in Errors	10.3%
Reduction in Product Lead Time	5.8%
Increase in Inventory Turnover	7.2%
Reduction in Quality Cost	9.0%
Increased Customer Satisfaction	2.5%
Decline in Complaints	11.6%
Increase in Market Share	13.7%
Increase in Sales Per Employee	8.6%
Increase in Return on Assets	1.3%

Figure 1.1 The impact of total quality management. (*Source*: Government Accounting Office, Washington, D.C.)

From this report it is understood that for the companies surveyed, while they are being successful at increasing product reliability (+11.3%), reducing complaints (−11.6%), and shortening processing times (−12%), return on assets (ROA) as an indication of profitability, has not kept pace. If those companies who have implemented TQM better than anyone else only increased profitability on the average of 1.3% something must be wrong.

If companies are going to be successful implementing TQM programs, there must be some connection between the measurements being improved (such as reliability, complaint reduction and processing time) and the impact on return on assets. If the major problem in dealing with profit is product quality, then no matter how it is defined, if product quality goes up then profitability must follow.

A certain regional director of maintenance for a major computer manufacturer was faced with a problem customer. The customer's perception was that the first time to repair (FTTR) and mean time between failure (MTBF) figures were unacceptable and if they were not fixed the account would be in jeopardy. Fortunately, the regional director had the presence of mind to gain the customers perspective first and to determine whether it resembled reality. It was discovered that the customer had been working with perceptions gained from problems which occurred three years earlier. The problems had been resolved since then and yet the perception remained. If any money had been spent increasing the quality of the maintenance services offered and not the customer's perception, profitability would have moved down. Even worse would be the impact on future sales through the loss of a customer. It must be understood that in order for profits to improve, companies must improve the right things.

To improve the right things a real problem pertaining to the profitability of the company must be solved. And, for all companies, once a problem has been solved and an increase in profitability occurs, the same solutions will not continue to reap the same benefits indefinitely. Since every solution serves to invalidate itself over time those indicators being improved today which result in an increase in profit may not result in an increase tomorrow. This can be quite a dilemma.

Many companies, after going through a full TQM program, are disappointed at the resulting profitability picture. It seems that the primary reason may be that the measurements and focusing mechanisms used to determine what needs to be improved may not have lead them to create a corresponding increase in profit. Many improvements may have resulted in merely increasing the potential of increasing profitability.

· · ·

Indeed, there are Malcolm Baldrige Award winners who are having tremendous financial problems.

· · ·

In January, 1992, the Wallace Co., famous for winning the Malcolm Baldrige Quality award in 1990 and based in Houston, Texas, filed for Chapter 11 bankruptcy protection.

There are also many companies who have implemented TQM and have had increases in profits. The Motorola Corporation and others, such as Xerox, have made advances in profitability through the implementation of TQM. According to the Motorola University their successes have also been spread to other companies not affiliated with Motorola. Their "secret weapon" is attributed to their cycletime reduction program. As cycletimes are reduced by eliminating non-value added activities quality problems seem to go away and costs begin to decline as employees leave through attrition. While this method has been proven to be successful, the biggest complaint is that it is very time consuming, taking long periods of time and investment before the effects in profitability are seen. Most CEOs do not have the patience.

The TQM II Concept

The key issue is not whether TQM works. There are too many companies who have been successful to say that it doesn't. But can it be improved? Can it be made to work faster, gain more profits, or continue beyond current management strategies to solve problems for which solutions are not readily available? And, just as importantly, can it be made so that more companies can duplicate it?

• • •

What is needed is a method to increase the probability that when an action is taken to improve it will have a positive impact on profitability as well as the overall health of the company.

• • •

What would be the impact if a program were developed which could systematically identify those things which, if improved, would result in an immediate increase in profit. And, if placed end to end, would create a process of "continuous profit improvement". This book is an attempt to document such a system. It represents the implementation of Total Quality Management utilizing the focusing mechanism provided by Dr. Eli Goldratt's Theory of Constraints (Goldratt, 1984). This concept has been named TQM II and represents the next phase in Total Quality Management.

TQM II: AN OVERVIEW

TQM II represents a tremendous change in direction for most companies. It introduces fundamental principles upon which to build a profitable foundation for any company, regardless of industry, including:

- A new measuring system.
- A process of "continuous profit improvement".
- A fundamental decision process focusing on global rather than local issues.
- A new method for analyzing the relationships between resources and determining where to focus efforts.
- New insights into how to use the traditional TQM tools to maximize profitability.
- New methods of scheduling the factory which have been proven to be superior to Just-in-Time.
- New methods for analyzing policy problems and arriving at simple solutions.

The initial thrust of this book will be to develop insight into the fundamental changes which must be addressed and then expanding them into the traditional tools provided by the engineering/quality sciences while providing a logical framework for managing the overall structure of the program. The objective is to create a solution to the traditional approach of TQM so that it is more in line with the goal of the company, which is to make money.

2
Creating the Process of "Continuous Profit Improvement"

In this chapter a new set of measurements designed to facilitate the improvement process as well as a process of "continuous profit improvement" are created.

OBJECTIVES

- To establish absolute measurements from which to judge the impact of *any* improvement process.
- To determine where to focus overall improvement objectives.
- To define the process of "continuous profit improvement".
- To gain insight on what type of problems will prevent improvement in profitability.

ESTABLISHING NEW MEASUREMENTS

Before any discussion of improvement can be entertained a method of measurement which can be agreed upon by all parties must be identified. To say an improvement has occurred requires validation. Most would agree that Return on Investment is an adequate measurement for determining whether an improvement has occurred. However, it does not provide insight into where to focus to produce improvements.

Due to an increase in competition over the past 10 years additional measurements were developed to deal with actions which were designed to increase a company's competitiveness. The key indicators became the competitive edge issues of quality, lead time and price. It was easy to develop a logical approach which would maximize each of these issues. Efforts were made to eliminate those things which contribute negatively. This fell into place with the current concepts of cost/waste reduction. However, what is being realized is that increasing a company's position with respect to the competitive edge issues may only serve to increase the potential for making more money. It does not guarantee increased profitability and when approached without benefit of a thorough understanding of the impact of the total corporate environment may result in a much less competitive entity.

What is needed is a new set of measurements and a process of improvement which, when implemented correctly, will guarantee that profitability will go up. If this new set of measurements can be agreed on, then what is left is to determine the relationship between these measurements and the corporate environment. Our decision processes and actions with regard to the process of *on-going improvement* should fall naturally from there.

For a decision system to work there must be a direct correlation between the measurements used externally, such as net profit (NP) and return on investment (ROI), and those used internally. This is obvious. What is being proposed and gaining more and more acceptance as the measurements of choice are:

```
Throughput (T)    - The rate at which the system generates
                    money through sales.

Inventory (I)     - All the money invested in purchasing the
                    things the system intends to sell.

Operating (O/E) - All the money the system spends in turning
Expense           Inventory into Throughput.
```

Throughput is represented by the formula sales minus raw material. Inventory includes any physical inventories such as work in process, finished goods and raw material but also includes tools, buildings, capital equipment and furnishings. Operating Expense includes expenditures such as direct and indirect labor, supplies, outside contractors and interest payments.

These measurements are understood by most people without hesitation. The objective is to maximize Throughput while minimizing Inventory and Operating Expense. They also relate directly to the way in which global goal attainment is measured.

```
Net Profit =  Throughput - Operating Expense

Return on Investment = Throughput - Operating Expense
                       ─────────────────────────────
                                Inventory
```

They can be used to describe any number of additional measurements which may give insight to their importance as a decision tool.

```
Productivity =      Throughput
                 Operating Expense

Inventory turns = Throughput
                  Inventory
```

Once established, these measurements can now be used to analyze the impact of each internal decision on the external measurements of NP and ROI. Whenever a decision is made the question becomes whether or not Throughput will go up or Inventory and Operating Expense will go down. Typical decisions include; where and how to focus process improvement efforts, what products should be sold and for what price, should a setup be torn down to run a hot order, and if so what should I charge the customer? Each of these decisions can be analyzed based on their impact on the key measurements of Throughput, Inventory and Operating Expense. If rework is reduced in a specific work center will Throughput go up? If so by how much? Will Inventory and Operating Expense go down? If so by how much?

What is needed next is an understanding of the environment dictating the effect on each measurement. In short, what are the occurrences in our environment which impact the creation of Throughput, and the existence of Inventory and Operating Expense?

DECIDING WHERE TO FOCUS

Most people would agree intuitively, that if given only one choice of what to improve in the three measurements that Throughput should be chosen the most important. However, beyond simple intuition are some very convincing issues:

- Inventory and Operating Expense are limited in their ability to be improved, since they both cannot be reduced past zero and a certain amount of each is absolutely required to produce and to protect Throughput.
- A process of "continuous profit improvement" based on a program which concentrates on a reduction of Operating Expense seems rather unlikely. It would be difficult to maintain. The closer to the objective of zero Operating Expense, the more difficult it becomes to continue. If the objective is actually met then sales would also be reduced to zero.
- If Inventory and Operating Expense exist to produce and protect the Throughput figure understanding more about what is to be done to improve Throughput becomes a prerequisite to dealing with the other two measurements.
- Throughput is not inherently limited and therefore produces the greatest opportunity for improvement. A tremendous number of Inventory and Operating Expense "sins" can be forgiven if the Throughput figure continuously grows at a fast enough pace.
- Concentrating on Throughput provides a tremendous leveraging effect in that since it is created by an interdependent sequence of events, very few things must be improved for Throughput to increase.

CHAPTER 2

The 99 to 1 Rule

Whenever the demand for two resources in a chain of events have reached 100% capacity, as in the following illustration, the probability is very high that sometimes the first resource will not be able to deliver to the second.

```
     100%  100%  Load
*----*----*----*
     25    25     Demand in Units
```

If this occurs then the second resource will not be able to deliver its demand either. However, capacity is usually described as an average capability distributed along a bell curve. The probability is very high that the first resource will constantly deliver less than 25 units. Since this is the case the probability is also very high that the second resource will rarely be loaded at 100% capacity. It will not have all the material necessary to keep it busy.

• • •

This means that in any chain of events there can be only one weakest link and if improvement is to occur only that link needs to be strengthened.

• • •

This is an advantage in determining where to focus. The 80/20 rule of the Pareto principle where 80% of the cost is created by 20% of the cost drivers is now changed to the 99/1 rule where 1% of the change has 99% of the impact.

The Impact on Corporate Functions

Since Throughput is described as the rate at which money enters the company all functions must be described by a rate; the rate at which parts are purchased; the rate at which designs are created; the rate at which products are sold. Any time a rate is established capacity must also be considered; the capacity to buy parts; the capacity to design; and the capacity to sell.

• • •

This means that not only are the physical resources subject to the laws governing probability and statistical fluctuation, but also the individual functions of a corporation.

• • •

If the ability to deliver is limited by capacity in production then an increase in the ability to sell will do nothing to increase the rate at which Throughput enters the company. This phenomenon offers a very distinct advantage in that very few things must improve in order for Throughput to go up.

THE NEED TO DEFINE THE PROCESS OF "CONTINUOUS PROFIT IMPROVEMENT"

A process of improvement should include a sequence of steps where at the end an improvement in a company's position relative to its goal of profitability should occur. This process, when repeated should produce a sequence of improvements. When repeated endlessly, it should produce a process of "continuous profit improvement". The 14 points so thoughtfully provided by Dr. Deming were never meant to fulfill the requirement as a sequence of steps, but rather a comprehensive structure for organizing the TQM program and has brought about tremendous change.

1. Have constancy of purpose
2. Adopt a new philosophy
3. Eliminate dependence on mass inspection
4. Cease price-alone purchasing
5. Plan constant improvement
6. Improve job training
7. Provide a higher level of supervision
8. Eliminate unsuitable material
9. Drive out fear by encouraging two-way communication
10. Get rid of numerical goals and slogans
11. Examine closely the impact of numerical standards
12. Teach and utilize statistical techniques
13. Institute a vigorous training program in new skills
14. Institutionalize the above points

Shewhart's concept of "plan-do-check-action" begs the obvious question, "what should be planned"? Of all the activities of a company, those that should be elevated to the highest priority should be those that pertain to making money. Unless a process of improvement can be defined which can predictably accomplish this, then improvements in profitability will be a hit-or-miss proposition.

DEFINING THE PROCESS STEPS

A process of improvement for Throughput will not automatically assume that the location of the weak link is known. If something is acting to restrict the amount of Throughput being generated then the first step should be to identify it. Once the weak link has been identified steps must be taken to insure that the amount of Throughput being generated is maximized through its proper use. There are two issues:

- The amount of available capacity at the weak link to apply to generating Throughput.
- The characteristics of the other resources which can be applied to insure that the weak link is not restricted in any way.

Figure 2.1 represents a chain of events in which resource 1 is the gating operation. Each resource feeds the next until reaching resource 4. The capacity of each resource is different and refers to its delivery capability in units. From this figure it is easy to see that the output limitation for this line is 25 units. It is also easy to see that in order to increase Throughput only resource 3's capability needs to be addressed. So, the improvement process must begin there.

Before simply buying another resource 3 it may be more profitable to see how much additional productive time can be gained from that resource as it currently exists. It may be found that resource 3's capability can be increased without buying a new resource. Maximizing the amount of productive time at the weak link may include:

- Creating a schedule for the weak link which uses every available minute of its time effectively.
- Selling a product mix into the market which maximizes the amount of Throughput generated.
- Reducing the amount of setup and maintenance time to maximize resource availability.

Once a strategy for delivering the maximum amount of Throughput from resource 3 has been developed this strategy must be protected. It is the other resources within the system and their characteristics which supply this capability. If resource 2, for whatever reason, did not deliver all of resource 3's parts requirements it would limit the number of units being created. If resource 3 was an NC machine and needed programs to run but the engineers were not delivering on time, Throughput would suffer. On the other hand, if all resources were to work at 100% efficiency and utilization the amount of Inventory in front of resources 2 and 3 would begin to climb. The result would be that return on investment would decrease, lead times would be expanded, and, eventually, Inventory would block the

```
Resource     1     2     3     4
             *----*----*----*
Capacity    70    60    25    40   =   25 Units
```

Figure 2.1 Chain of events.

creation of Throughput. So, all non-constraint resources including functional organizations such as sales, engineering and quality should deliver to the constraint what is needed for it to maximize the creation of Throughput and nothing more.

After maximizing its capability and insuring that all other resources are delivering to resource 3 what it needs, another strategy must now be adopted to increase the amount of Throughput generated—the addition of another resource 3.

In the following figure resource 3 has been elevated by purchasing another machine and doubling its capability. The assembly line is now capable of producing at the rate of 40 units.

```
Resource     1    2    3    4
             *----*----*----*
Capacity    70   60   50   40   =   40 Units
```

Notice that when this occurs, the weak link has moved and is now in another location. It becomes obvious for a process of continuous improvement that Throughput must now be maximized on a different resource and that all other resources must be aware of those requirements for protecting the new weak link. To make a further improvement capacity at resource 4 must then be increased. Because of this change occurring, everything about the company has changed such as where to focus improvements and how to support the new weak link. This must be considered each time a weak link has been elevated.

The process of improvement for Throughput is:
- Identify the weak link or "Constraint".
- Determine how to maximize it's capability to produce Throughput, or, "Exploit" it.
- Determine what to do with all other resources to support the Constraint, "Subordinate".
- Strengthen the weak link, "Elevate".
- "Repeat" the process.

Note: It is important to remember that when the weak link has been strengthened that there is a tendency to continue to use the same solutions even though the weak link has moved and the solutions have become obsolete—Avoid "Inertia".

• • •

This process is not to be confused with the Shewhart's "Plan-Do-Check-Action". In any chain of events, only one thing must be fixed to increase Throughput.

• • •

IDENTIFYING THE WEAK LINK

Whenever decisions are made from a global perspective, the alternatives are determined by the limitations of the system and not by an isolated, localized algorithm. To know where to focus to make an improvement means that the limitations and their impact must be known. This raises the question of what must be done to determine the limitations of the system.

By definition unless the company is making an infinite amount of money there must be a weak link. How should it be identified and what are the elements which limit the weak link's ability to perform to its maximum? Weak links are categorized in a number of different ways; market, material, managerial, capacity, logistical and behavioral, each having their own impact on the smooth operation of the company. Logistical constraints involve limitations placed on the system by the planning and control systems. Managerial constraints are erroneous management strategies, policies and decision mechanisms. Behavioral constraints are those behaviors exhibited by employee work habits which result in poor performance from a global perspective.

Behavioral Constraints

Behavior is the result of an attempt to act or react, in a logical way, to the environment and specific situations encountered. It is directly effected by the training, education, measurement systems, experiences, attitudes and mental dispositions of the people involved. Whenever a behavior is in conflict with reality and results in a negative impact on the global measurements of the company it is said to be a behavioral constraint. Behavioral constraints are caused by a number of different reasons. Probably the most prevalent cause is linked to the measurement system. *Tell me how you will measure me, I will tell you how I will behave.* Whether implicit or explicit, the measurement systems will dictate the way in which people act. The best example of this is the concept of *staying busy.*

One of the hardest behaviors to change is the concept that resources must stay busy, and yet it may be one of the more devastating. The assumption is made that whatever an employee does to stay busy will result in good things happening. It is reinforced by the utilization measurement where every resource must be highly utilized or the company will lose money. This concept is held by management and employees alike, although not necessarily for the same reasons. The extended result of this kind of behavior is that inventories begin to climb, product mixes become unbalanced, schedules are slipped and material shortages occur.

Another example of a behavioral constraint is in the setup savings tendency. Combining setup without the knowledge of the global impact on Throughput, Inventory and Operating Expense may result in a decline in profitability. When viewed from a global perspective it may seem almost irrational and the impact on profitability often predictable. And yet it is very difficult to convince a foreman to stop.

Managerial Constraints

Poor management policies often act to restrict the ability to maximize the utilization of physical resources or to prevent the proper use of non-constraint resources in protecting the creation of Throughput. As an example, a policy of setting commission schedules for sales representatives using activity based accounting to determine which products to push into the market may cause the poor exploitation of resources for maximizing profitability. It may, in fact, cause serious damage to profitability, and yet was imposed by management. A policy of establishing quality cost as the mechanism for focusing improvement may result in money spent to improve an area which will not help to increase the overall profitability of the company. (See Chapter five on Correcting the Decision Process). *We are a defense contractor* means that the market may be the limitation and the only way to change this is to change the mind of the board of directors.

Capacity Constraints

Any time the demand placed on a resource exceeds it's available capacity it is said to be a capacity constraint. Capacity constraints can include machines or people and restrict the creation of Throughput. Primary constraints are those which restrict the output of the entire company. Secondary constraints restrict the ability to properly subordinate to the primary constraint. In other words, if the demand placed on a resource increases to the point where the probability is low that it will be able to deliver to the primary constraint what is needed, it is said to be a secondary capacity constraint.

Market Constraints

Perhaps the most important constraints to consider are those offered by the market. The market controls the product, pricing, lead time, quantity and quality of the goods and services demanded, and it establishes the necessary conditions for creating Throughput. Whenever market demand is less than the capability of the company's resources a market constraint exists. While market constraints have many causes, most exist due to management policies.

Logistical Constraints

Anytime problems occur which originate from the planning and control systems within the company, it is said to be a logistical constraint. Material requirements planning systems which are capacity insensitive create problems in the proper synchronization of resources and can escalate the amount of Inventory and production problems which exist. A cumbersome purchasing process, such as selecting the lowest price from a minimum of three bids from three different vendors for every purchase, may actually restrict the creation of Throughput.

Necessary Conditions

A growing number of companies are being required by their vendors to implement statistical process control. If this demand is not met they will be discontinued as approved vendors. Necessary conditions are boundaries or demands placed on companies, departments or individuals, originating internally or externally, which serve to regulate activity. They may include government regulations such as environmental issues involving the disposal of toxic waste, customer demands or moral issues such as honesty. Management may place necessary conditions on employees. Stock holders place necessary conditions on companies for the purchase of stock. Whenever the necessary condition is not being met there are usually serious implications. If a necessary condition of employment is honesty and the employee is caught stealing then he or she will probably be fired. If a necessary condition for being in business is adequate cash flow and it is not present then the company will probably go bankrupt. Necessary conditions should be distinguished from constraints. A necessary condition can become a constraint unless the condition is met. Once met, any improvement in it will not continue to improve the profit position of the company. However, it must be continually enforced.

The Cost Mentality

Most of the irrational behavior exhibited in companies originates from a "cost mentality". The cost mentality results in the tendency to optimize local measurements at the expense of global measurements. In most companies, there seems to be almost a natural tendency to departmentalize organizations and to develop measurements which optimize the results at a local level. The use of local measurements has been taught in the business schools for decades and further reinforced in the business world. However, unless an improvement in the local measurements are supported by a positive global impact then the local measurement system must be viewed as invalid. The cost mentality is the basis for most constraints and is probably our biggest enemy.

3

Dealing With the Physical Environment

Chapter three begins the process of understanding how to address problems associated with the physical environment and what the global impacts of those problems will be from a profitability perspective.

OBJECTIVES

- To understand how resources interface and the resulting impact on the system (product flow).
- To begin to understand the impact of physical limitations from a global perspective.
- To begin to understand what the impact to currently accepted technology will be and how to change them.
- To understand how and where to focus physical improvements.
- To introduce the concept of the *diagnostic system* and to understand the problems inherently provided by current information systems technology on the ability to identify physical limitations.

IMPROVING IN THE DEPENDENT VARIABLE ENVIRONMENT

Any attempt to improve the performance of constrained resources must begin with the right question. In addressing the alternatives it is important not to be misdirected by preconceived notions of what activities will be necessary. An improvement just to improve may actually reduce profitability. The question which should be asked is, *how can the Throughput of the company be increased given the current situation*? Properly framed, the question can be properly answered.

In any chain of events, each link within the chain is capable of impacting any other link. It is the characteristics of the links and their relative position within the

17

chain which dictate how each must interact with the other and determines the overall effectiveness of the system.

One resource can negatively affect another by:

- Not delivering.
- Delivering late.
- Delivering poor quality.
- Delivering incorrect products.
- Delivering too early.

Each resource will also have variation in these effects. A resource may sometimes deliver the right product on time or deliver a high quality product as well. It is the characteristics of each resource which dictate its ability to cope with what it has received or which may improve or make worse the position of the next. A resource which has additional capacity to deal with a rework problem is in a much better position than a resource which has no additional capacity at all. Understanding this issue, while it may seem very simple, has had far reaching impact on the overall TQM program in it's ability to focus as well as manage improvement.

• • •

The dependent variable environment is the environment where resources are dependent on each other in their capability to produce and are subject to variation in that capability.

• • •

UNDERSTANDING PRODUCT FLOW

Creating the Product Flow Diagram

While constraints may come in many different flavors, to begin to understand the relationships between resources and then to predict the specific impact each resource will have on the overall system, it is necessary to understand how products flow through the factory. The product flow diagram is a detailed description of the product flow and the resources involved in the production operation. It is a cornerstone to organizing any TQM program and is somewhat different from the process flow diagram in that primary interest is placed on determining the sequence of operations and the resources which are used. Emphasis on storage or transportation is ignored.

The basic building block of the product flow diagram is the part/operation or *station*. The station is an operation being performed on a specific part. It is the correct sequencing of these stations plus the addition of the resource upon which the operation is performed which creates the product flow diagram. In figure 3.1

Indented Bill of Material			Routing Part	Op.	Res.
123		Make	123	10	R-4
	124	**Make**		20	R-5
		125 Purch		30	R-6
	126	Make	**124**	**10**	**R-3**
		127 Purch		20	R-2
				30	R-1
			126	10	R-3
				20	R-2
				30	R-1

Stations List	Resource Load	
123/30 R-6	R-1	100%
123/20 R-5	R-2	75%
123/10 R-4	R-3	50%
124/30 R-1	R-4	70%
124/20 R-2	R-5	90%
124/10 R-3	R-6	60%
125/Purch		
126/30 R-1		
126/20 R-2		
126/10 R-3		
127/Purch		

Figure 3.1 The basic building blocks.

the indented bill of material shows which parts are used on what assembly operations. The routing shows the operations which must be performed, the sequencing and the resources involved for each part. The stations list shows all the different stations which are created by combining the bill of material and routing file into one structure. Also included is resource load information.

Notice that in the routing part number 124's first operation is operation 10 on resource R-3 (in bold). The station in the stations list is therefore 124/10 (in bold).

When creating a visual diagram, stations are combined using arrows to define the production flow. Arrows designate the direction of flow to and from specific stations. Stations which have more than one arrow converging are assembly operations or *convergent* operations (Figure 3.2).

Stations/Resources 124/30/R-1 and 126/30/R-1, which are the last steps in creating parts 124 and 126, feed Station/Resource 123/10/R-4.

Convergent

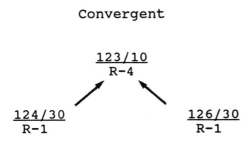

Figure 3.2 Convergent operations.

Stations which have multiple out-going arrows are *divergent* operations (Figure 3.3). Material flowing from station 1234/10 diverges to stations 1245/30 and 1267/30. Converging and diverging operations cause unique problems under certain circumstances to be seen later in this chapter.

The product flow diagram creates the chain of events for the production process. In this way it is understood what stations occur before and after each other within the chain.

Based on the route file, bill of material file and resource load presented the product flow diagram would look like figure 3.4.

Notice that at the top of the structure the last part/operation is being performed and at the bottom raw material enters. In this manner it is easy to construct the chain of events occurring within the factory from the beginning to the end for each order created by the customer.

The Impact of Capacity

Whenever the capacity/demand of each resource is added a better picture is created for determining where to focus to maximize the global impact. Resources which are particularly vulnerable are those which have been loaded at or near capacity. These resources should be given close attention during the improvement process. However, it is equally important, although not as obvious, to insure that

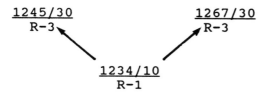

Figure 3.3 Divergent operations.

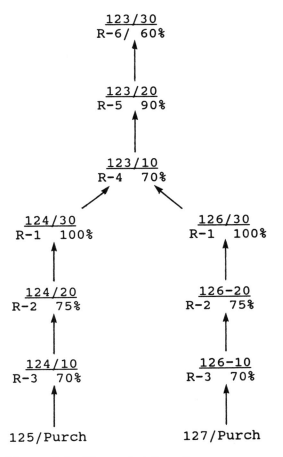

Figure 3.4 The product flow diagram.

once a product has passed the constraint it will not be scrapped or require rework which absorbs constraint time. The chain of resources which leads from stations 124/30 and 126/30, (performed on resource R-1) to station 123/30 (performed on resource R-6) must be very well protected from scrap problems. Rework problems occurring on station 123/10, performed on resource R-4 and loaded at 70%, cause less of a problem than those rework problems occurring at station 123/20, performed on resource R-5 and loaded at 90%.

In the *process* flow diagram emphasis is placed on increasing the efficiency of how resources interface or reducing waste. A highly questionable approach from a global perspective. In the *product* flow diagram the issue is to increase or protect the creation of Throughput. A closer look at the impact of product flow is made in chapter eleven on the implementation of Statistical Process Control.

IMPROVING PERFORMANCE ON CONSTRAINED RESOURCES

Techniques for increasing constrained resource capacity at a local level deal with the different categories of resource time including; processing time, setup time, and idle time. The objective is to convert setup and idle time to processing time and to minimize the processing time required.

THE QUICK SETUP (SMED) STRATEGY

The SMED Process

Originally conceived and documented by Dr. Shigeo Shingo, the Single Minute Exchange of Die (SMED) strategy is a mandatory technique under the small lot size production strategy. Over a nineteen year period Dr. Shingo had created a technique which drastically reduced the amount of setup time required in production by implementing a three stage process of:

- "Separating internal from external setup".
- "Converting internal to external setup".
- "Streamlining all aspects of the setup operation".

The internal setup (IED) describes those operations which are performed while the process is stopped. External setup or (EOD) describes those operations which are performed while the machine is running.

The first stage in this process is to identify and separate those things which are normally done while the process is stopped and those things which are normally done while the process is running. A large amount of time during setup, as much as 30–50%, is usually spent on tasks which can be done while the machine is running, but due to poor organization are done while the machine is offs, such as trying to find essential parts, jigs or fixtures. A specific tool may be needed to move a fixture onto or remove a fixture from a specific machine. This same tool may be used by other machines and operators in similar setup operations on numerous machines. However, unless it is at the proper location at the proper time and in proper working order, it is useless. Stopping the constraint to hunt for the right fixture or tool can be disastrous. The loss is equal to the Throughput loss of the chain. If only one chain exists, then it will be for Throughput of the entire corporation. An implementation of step one would be to insure that everything needed to accomplish the setup is available at the machine when it is shut down. Checklists are developed which itemize the requirements, function checks are made to determine if fixtures are in working order and the movement of material and fixtures to and from machines is streamlined and accomplished while the machine is running.

The second stage is to convert those things which are normally done while the machine is down so that they can be done while the machine is running. If stopping the constraint will result in such a great loss everything possible must be done prior to this event occurring to minimize the amount of down time there will be. There are two issues; converting those things which were assumed to be internal by re-examining their function and identifying those things which can be converted by a process change. The utilization of dual purpose dies where one die may fit a number of different products means that product changes can be accomplished without the need of stopping the operation.

The third stage is to further reduce the amount of setup by reducing the time required to perform the internal tasks remaining. In some cases this may include radical process changes, in others it may include small changes such as shortening the amount of turns required on a bolt or replacing the bolt with a clamp. A large amount of time is spent studying the internal setup process for function. Individual steps are examined to determine whether they are required based on the actual function that must be done and, if not, eliminated or modified. For example, in some machining operations clamps are used requiring a large number of bolts (as many as 15–20 or more) which must be removed each time the clamp is removed. Each bolt may take a relatively long time to remove. In this case, shortening the bolt will not be a satisfactory solution because the strength of the overall clamp would be impaired by the use of shorter bolts. An examination of the function and assumptions made for each part of the clamping operation and a rethinking of the task to be performed may find that removing the bolts may not be required after all. By cutting a U-shaped hole in the side of the washer and modifying the bolt holes in the clamp so that they will fit over the bolt heads, the washers can be removed after one turn of the bolt and the clamp removed over the top of the bolt heads. There are two major issues; determining whether a function is required by examining the assumptions made and, if required, determining whether a task can be modified to accomplish the required function and how to modify it.

SMED Implementation

The method of SMED implementation varies from company to company including the implementation at all operations in support of the small lot size strategy, to improve at bottleneck operations so that production is increased, or to reduce cost. With respect to cost, priority is usually given to those resources requiring the greatest amount of time to setup or based on a cost of setup algorithm. However, in TQM II the third principle states that the value of an activity is determined by the limitations of the system (see chapter seven). So, the value of a setup reduction activity from a global perspective is directly linked to the specific limitation being addressed. If the setup is being reduced on a non-constraining resource, regardless of the cost implications, the impact may actually be negative on the profitability of the company. Figure 3.5 illustrates.

```
Setup Cost                                     Setup      Setup
Per Hour                                       Times      Quan.
                          A     B
   $10                *-----*----*-----*       A 3 hours  25/wk

                                               B 1 hour   10/wk
```

Figure 3.5 Setup cost.

Resource A feeds resource B and has a setup time of 3 hours at a cost of $10 per hour or $30 dollars per set up. Resource B's cost is also $10 per hour but for only one hour or $10 per setup. An engineer wants to spend $2,000 to eliminate the setup on resource A. Since resource A looses 75 hours per week to setup at ten dollars per hour or $750 he estimates that he will be able to recapture the $2,000 expenditure in 2.7 weeks. However, Figure 3.6 adds some crucial information usually not considered.

Resource A is a non-constraint resource with excess capacity loaded to 50% while resource B is the constraint loaded to 100%. Any reduction in setup time at resource A will only result in an increase in the amount of excess capacity available at that resource. The productivity model illustrates what is important.

$$\text{Productivity} = \frac{\text{Throughput}}{\text{Operating Expense}} = \frac{\text{No Change}}{\uparrow \$2,000}$$

From a global perspective Operating Expense is represented by money paid out to employees in the form of payroll, utilities such as water or electricity, rental for buildings or machines and employee benefits. It is highly unlikely that any one of these categories of expenses will decline through the reduction of setup time. No one is going to be laid off; the plant is not going to be reduced in size and employee benefits will not decline. However, if the $2,000 check is written Operating Expense will immediately increase by the $2,000. If Throughput does not go up productivity as well as profitability will decline.

If the engineer had spent money to increase the available capacity at resource B (just the opposite of the cost model), while Operating Expense still would not have declined, the amount of Throughput entering the company would have gone

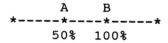

```
        A     B
  *-----*----*-----*
     50%   100%
```

Figure 3.6 The impact of product flow on setup.

up to offset the additional Operating Expense created by spending the $2,000.

As seen in the above illustration, implementing SMED to reduce cost is a poor focusing mechanism which can lead to a loss in profit. But, by focusing on bottleneck/constraint operations improvement can have an immediate positive effect.

· · ·

Bottlenecks occur any time the demand placed on a resource is equal to or more than capacity.

A constraint is anything which prevents the system from attaining its goal of making more money.

· · ·

Setup reduction programs should be planned to increase available time on the constraint resource(s) as part of the Exploitation phase and near constraint resources as part of the Subordination phase of the five step improvement process.

Avoiding Inertia

Many times resources become constrained for reasons not related to setup or process issues. Poor scheduling or resource utilization can create bottlenecks where none should exist. A misinterpretation of data can lead to setup reduction programs which have no impact or even a negative impact on the bottom line. An electronics manufacturer of communications equipment who was operating under JIT was busily increasing the efficiency at bottleneck operations so that Throughput would increase. The capacity report had indicated that several resources were scheduled at or well above capacity (83 to 144%). However, no overtime was being worked and the due date performance to the customer was at 98%—a good physical indication that the companies assumption of a physical constraint existing in production was invalid. Upon closer examination it was found that the real constraint to making more money was an inability to obtain sufficient raw material to release to the floor. A further examination found that purchasing was placing a high value on the reduced price of raw material and that products being received were being rejected at incoming inspection as being inadequate. Any time spent increasing the capacity of bottleneck resources at this facility at that time was a total waste. The only way of increasing Throughput at this facility at this time would be to change a policy in purchasing.

The resources which were considered bottlenecks may have been constraining Throughput at one time or another but were either improved or became non-constraining due to a new policy created in purchasing. It is very important to repeat the five step process once the constraint has been broken. However, it is sometimes not so easy to see when to do it.

CHAPTER 3

Creating Common Sense

The success of any SMED program has a direct relation to the ability to examine the underlying assumptions made in any operation. While it may be a worthwhile effort to examine the actual technology employed by Dr. Shingo, and others, in the implementation of SMED, it may be a better idea, and in the long run more profitable to examine the thought processes behind the creation of the solution. Common sense, it seems, has its birthplace in the ability to recognize the obvious from the not so obvious. What keeps people from recognizing those things which are obvious is that their thinking process is already shaped by pre-existing assumptions before the process begins. In the five step improvement process described earlier Inertia is caused by pre-existing assumptions. The electronics company described above may have started with a legitimate resource constraint but failed to start the process over again once it was broken and the constraint had moved to purchasing. What must be available to every worker, manager, and executive is the ability to examine any situation without the negative impact of pre-existing assumptions. This is the purpose of the Effect-Cause-Effect, Assumption Model and Positive Tree tools described in the policy analysis section of this book. This is why Dr. Shingo suggests as part of his setup reduction process that the function of each step and tool in the process be examined and re-defined. Breaking the underlying assumptions behind an activity or function gives rise to common sense. The new tools described in chapter four add a much needed dimension to the setup reduction program.

THE TOTAL PRODUCTIVE MAINTENANCE (TPM) STRATEGY

The TPM Process

The proper maintenance of equipment will have a major impact on the overall profitability of any company. According to Seeichi Nakajima in his book, *Total Productive Maintenance*, TPM involves a company wide effort to create a "fundamental improvement within a company by improving worker and equipment utilization" while maintaining a low Life Cycle Cost of maintenance. TPM is a system of maintenance for the entire life-span of the equipment to include Maintenance Prevention (designing equipment to be maintenance free), Preventive Maintenance (insuring that equipment remains in good working condition), Corrective Maintenance (repairing and re-engineering broken equipment), and Autonomous Maintenance (operator involvement). Attempts are made to eliminate the "big six losses" of equipment failure, setup and adjustment, idling and minor stoppages, reduced speed, process defects, and reduced yield. The effectiveness of the overall system is measured based on availability, efficiency and quality. Availability is determined by the formula.

```
Availability = Operation Time
               Available Time
```

Operation time refers to the net available time during the day minus equipment down time. Available time refers to the total time available in the day minus planned maintenance. Efficiency is determined by:

```
Efficiency = Net Operating Rate x Operating Speed Rate
```

The operating speed rate is determined by dividing the theoretical cycle time by the actual cycle time. The net operating rate is determined by the actual processing time divided by the operation time.

Quality is described in TPM as a function of the defect rate and is quantified by the following formula:

```
Defect Rate = Processed Amount - Defect Amount  x 100
                     Processed Amount
```

The TPM effectiveness rating formula is:

```
Effectiveness = Availability x Efficiency x Quality
```

In traditional TPM, the maintenance activity is focused based on the volume of occurrence. The resource with the lowest effectiveness rating is given the highest priority.

Although not mentioned in Seiichi's book, other indicators of system health include mean time between failure (MTBF) (the average time it takes for a machine to go from one failure to another), mean time to repair (MTTR) (the average time it takes to go from start to finish on a single repair), and its historical track record according to statistical process control (SPC)—can the process be controlled and how often does it require adjustment or repair. Under Maintenance Prevention, concentration should be on designing into the resources a high MTBF and low MTTR rating as well as quick setup strategies.

Changing the TPM Focus

In figure 3.7, under the traditional TPM approach, resource C with a 66% effectiveness rating is obviously the problem resource needing immediate attention. However, from a global perspective there are other things to consider. If resource

Res	Avail.	Eff.	Qual.	=	Effect Rating
A	90%	95%	97%		82%
B	90%	93%	95%		80%
*C	80%	92%	90%		66%

Figure 3.7   The TPM effectiveness rating.

A is the constraint and has an overall effectiveness rating of 82% this could very well be a critical problem and is not considered by the current TPM focusing mechanism. Figure 3.8 illustrates.

Resource A is loaded to 100%. Therefore, any loss of time on resource A results in a loss of Throughput which may never be recaptured. Any scrap results in a loss equal to the entire sales price (the cost of replacing the raw material due to scrap plus the Throughput amount lost by having to recreate the product on the constraint is equal to the sales price). This means that 18% of total sales would be lost forever. Resource B at 90% load should definitely be considered as the possible number two issue. Resource C is only 50% loaded and should be given a relative priority lower than the other two unless the problems of resource C will negatively impact products already passed to resource A. An additional impact of the Effectiveness rating is that by combining availability and efficiency measures with quality it masks a key issue and that is, depending on where in the process a quality issue hits, its level of importance may be magnified regardless of the amount of excess load available. If, in figure 3.7, the quality rating was the recorded scrap rate for each resource, there would be a cumulative effect resulting in the loss of 17% of total sales generated $[(.97 \times .95 \times .90) - 1)]$. This may be the most important issue to address.

The health indicators of a machine, regardless of current demand, will give an indication of problems which may impact Throughput at a later time. Poor health indicators should never be ignored regardless of their current impact. If a machine or group of machines which are loaded to 50% should suddenly breakdown for a period of time much longer than expected they could become temporary constraints and may block the Throughput of the entire company. Principle 5 states that the utilization of any resource may be determined by any other resource in a chain of events.

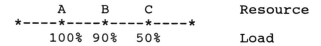

Figure 3.8   The impact of product flow on TPM.

Note: A poor machine rating is also an indicator that bad parts are getting into the system and could threaten the constraint(s).

After consideration for the dependent variable environmental issues, the global impact of the measurements involved in the above effectivity rating would be an immediate 15% decline in sales due to lost capacity from resource A $[(.90 \times .95 - 1)]$ and a 17% loss of sales due to scrap from resources A, B and C for a total of 32% loss of sales dollars which will never be recaptured. Inventory and Operating Expense would rise due to a lack of protective capacity on resource B. The order of importance might be to fix the scrap on resource C then the availability of resource A. Obviously the need exists to fix both.

As in the application of all the management sciences discussed so far, whenever a machines status interferes with the proper implementation of the five step improvement process its order of priority should be elevated above the normal level of activity. Additional insight is given to methods of focusing on those resources required in subordination through buffer management to be discussed later.

QUALITY FOCUS IN THE FACTORY

Where and how to focus a quality program into the factory is a matter of priorities, since reality is a function of the time and money available. If the necessary condition of good quality, as perceived by the customer, is not being fulfilled then priority must be given to solving this problem first. The Quality Function Deployment (QFD) program creates the relationship between the individual functional departments and the customer. The objective is to insure that those product attributes which are deemed unsatisfactory from the customers perspective are fixed by the appropriate organization (see chapter nine on Process/Product Design).

The next order of business is to determine what portion of the factory is the most vulnerable with respect to Throughput, Inventory and Operating Expense, and to strengthen and protect those areas. Obviously, if the resource which has been loaded to a greater extent than any other also has a quality problem, it must be dealt with immediately. This resource controls the Throughput being generated for a large portion of the company. Solving a quality problem here will immediately improve profitability.

However, several questions must be answered before knowing where and how to focus activities to improve and protect profitability.

- As indicated earlier, what would be the impact of solving a scrap problem at the constraint by spending $5,000 to buy a new fixture to increase the capability index (Cpk), (see chapter ten), only to find that the parts are being scrapped at a later operation?
- In addition, what would be the impact of quality problems which occur on resources which are loaded to near or secondary constraint levels?

- And finally, what would be the impact if the constraint or constraints processed material which was destined to be scrapped due to earlier operations or which had prerequisite measurement requirements from other resources which had not been met?

Problems on Resources Which Feed the Constraint

In figure 3.9 resources A, B and C are connected by operations which feed linearly from left to right. Resources A and C have been loaded to 50% and have scrap rates of 20% and 15% respectively. Resource B has been identified as the constraint, is loaded to 100% and has a scrap rate of 5%.

Whenever A scraps a part there will be a loss of the raw material involved. Additional material will be started at the gating operation to replace what has been lost. No one will be hired as a result of the scrap so the loss is the cost of raw material alone. However, the high scrap rate indicates that a severe problem exists in a resource which directly feeds the constraint. If scrap material absorbs processing time on the constraint Throughput will go down. While it may not be as high a priority to solve the scrap problem on resource A, it should be a very high priority to prevent, in any way possible, scrap material from being processed on resource B. If a method cannot be devised to screen out defective material then fixing resource A would command a high priority.

Dealing With Near Constraint Resources

Figure 3.10 is similar to figure 3.9 except that instead of scrap, rework is the issue. The load on resources A and C has also been changed as a result of the additional labor required to rework the parts. Resource A's load has been increased to 90% resulting in a high probability that A will be unable to deliver to B to meet B's schedule.

To insure that products which are to be processed on resource A will arrive at B on time, more processing time must be found for resource A. Under this condition material is released earlier to insure that parts can go from the gating operation to the constraint on time, resulting in an increase in Inventory, or overtime must be expended, resulting in an increase in Operating Expense. So, fixing the

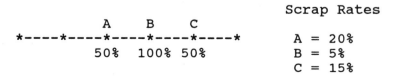

Figure 3.9 Problems on resources feeding the constraint.

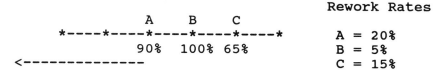

Figure 3.10   Near constraint resources.

rework on near constraint resources will result in a decrease in either inventory or operating expense, or both, and an increase in the protection of the constraining resource (B).

Secondary Constraints

In figure 3.10, if in trying to release material earlier on near constraint resources it is found that time zero (today) were to prevent being able to release material earlier (yesterday) then the rework would be responsible for creating the secondary constraint and a method must be devised for increasing available production time on resource A so that B can be protected. Secondary constraints also command a high priority.

Problems After the Constraint

Resource C, while it has a low utilization rate, processes material which has already been through the constraint. As seen earlier, whenever a part is scrapped here there is a loss of raw material since additional material must be started as replacements and there is a loss of constraint time. The time from the constraint used to create the part did not result in the generation of Throughput. In this case, fixing the scrap on resource C would also command a high priority.

But what is the impact of rework which occurs after the constraint? In the following figure resource B has a rework problem which has driven the load to near constraint levels at 90%. When this occurs additional capacity must be found to insure that orders will be made on time. The net result is that sales orders will be pushed out and therefore arrive late to the customer.

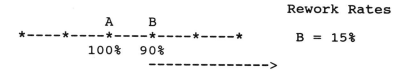

Fixing resource B's problem would result in less inventory between A and the end of the process and less operating expense used to support the overtime required to ship on time.

The Aggregation of Resource Capacity

Seldom will any manufacturing facility have only one resource. And so, when considering what must be fixed it is the aggregation or total resource capability which untimately determines the priority. In other words, just because a resource is loaded to 85% does not mean it automatically gets attention. The following illustration suggests a new perspective is necessary.

```
 A    B    C    D            Rework Rates
 *----*----*----*
85%  30%  50% 100%             A = 15%
```

Resources A, B, C and D represent a chain of resources in a production process which feeds from resource A through to resource D. Resource D is the constraint while resource A because of a rework problem is loaded to near constraint levels, 85%, and may have problems associated with an insufficient amount of capacity. But the question in the process described above is, will resource D be threatened with a lack of material arriving from A? Since the objective here is to insure that D is used continuously in the production of Throughput this question must be answered. Obviously, resource B will have problems in that it may not have enough available capacity but, should money be spent to fix it? By looking at resource A from a local perspective it would appear that it needs to be fixed. But, what is the global impact? Since the objective is to arrive at D on time the impact of available capacity on all resources in front of D must be considered not just A. So, the question must be rephrased to read what is the impact of available capacity on resources A, B and C in being able to deliver to D on time? With this in mind the excess capacity available at B and C must be considered in its ability to overcome any problems which may occur at A. This is the subject of buffer management and is discussed in chapter six on improving on just in time.

Conclusion

The most vulnerable portions of the factory with respect to quality and from a global perspective include:

- The primary and secondary constraint(s).
- The string of resources leading from the constraint(s) to the end of the process.

- The material being fed to the constraint or constraints.
- Near-Constraint resources whose problems cannot be overcome by capacity at other resources.

Note: Additional methods for increasing capacity on constrained resources include design/redesign of products and processes, statistical process control and design of experiments and is discussed in later chapters.

• • •

If the constraint to making more money does not exist in production, no amount of setup reduction or decreased machine down time will increase Throughput and the chances are very great that a decrease in Operating Expense will also not occur

• • •

THE IMPACT OF PRODUCT FLOW ON THE SCHEDULING PROCESS

The relative positioning of constraints and non-constraints will have a large impact on the way the organization performs, the problems which will surface, and the decisions which must be made regarding the TQM/SPC program. How a plant should be scheduled and the actions of workers and managers is directly impacted by the way in which product flows through the factory. Certain situations with respect to the location of constraint and non-constraint resources will cause workers and managers to react in a predictable manner which will have a negative effect on profitability. Correcting these problems is imperative and is a primary tenant of the Drum-Buffer-Rope process discussed in chapter six, Improving On Just-In-Time. The following is a synopsis of the situations which will occur and the resulting impact.

Constraints feeding constraints

```
Gating                    100%        100%        Sales
Operations       ---*-----*-----*-----*------* Order
                                      90%
```

Whenever constraints of equal capacity occur in sequence the first resource will be the primary constraint due to an inability for it to adequately feed the second.

The load will rarely be at maximum on the second constraint. However, the amount of protection required to insure that the sales order due dates will be met is greater and the predictiveness of sales order delivery will be lower. Obviously improvement programs would focus on maximizing the amount of Throughput which can be gained from the primary constraint and on increasing the amount of protective capacity available from the other. Fortunately, this situation does not exist in reality very often. Because of the problems it creates, companies usually elevate one or the other.

Constraints feeding non-constraints

```
Gating                    100%    50%         Sales
Operations        ---*------*------*------*  Order
```

   When the constraint feeds a non-constraint operation the non-constraint may be idle for long periods of time. The correct response in this case is to maximize the efficiency and utilization of the constraint while subordinating those requirements of the non-constraint to whatever the constraint needs. However, the general tendency is to attempt to work the non-constraint at high efficiency and utilization as well due to an invalid measuring system, whether explicit or implicit. Since this is an impossibility, managers will tend to reshape the environment by moving the constraint to increase the desired measurements. Constraints should be manipulated based on the desired impact on Throughput, Inventory and Operating Expense and not to increase the efficiencies and utilization of non-constraint resources.

Non-Constraints feeding constraints

```
Gating                    50%   100%         Sales
Operations        *------*------*------*  Order
```

   As long as traditional measurements are used in this situation the non-constraint resource will tend to be over-utilized. Since there is no restriction to incoming material it can keep producing. Unfortunately, overall output is controlled by the constraint. Inventories build and Operating Expense increases as a result. As inventories build additional bottlenecks are created requiring overtime.

Non-constraints feeding non-constraints

```
Gating                    50%    50%         Sales
Operations        ---*------*------*------*  Order
```

Whenever a non-constraint feeds a non-constraint the tendency will be to maximize the efficiency and utilization of each resulting in an increase in Inventory and Operating Expense and decreasing Throughput. Non-constraints should only be utilized when necessary to feed constraints or in the creation of Throughput.

Non-constraints and constraints feeding assembly operations (Convergent)

```
                          A       C
                         100%    Asmb         Sales
Gating          ---*-----*------*------* Order
Operations                      |
                ---*-----*------*
                         50%
                          B
```

In convergent operations regardless of whether a constraint is involved, the tendency is to maximize the utilization of all resources by the utilization of large lot sizes, The result is that material will move through the facility in waves. Resources will be overloaded one minute and empty of work the next.

In cases where one leg of the convergence is restricted, as in the illustration, the overutilization of the non-constraint will force work in process to increase in the assembly operation while under protection of the non-constraint leg will leave material arriving from the constraint leg sitting in assembly without matching parts. Resource A is the constraint with 100% load while resource B is the non-constraint at 50%. Over utilizing resource B will cause material to collect in resource C which cannot go further without parts from A. However, parts arriving from resource A should not be kept waiting at resource C for matching parts from resource B.

Non-constraints and constraints feeding more than one operation (Divergent).

```
                 A       B
Gating          ---*-----*------*------* Downstream
Operations               |              Operations
                    ------*------*
                          C
```

Whenever there is a divergence in the delivery of material there is an opportunity for misallocation. Material which should have been used to fill one order was used on another or went into stock. Material flowing from resource A diverges and is sent to resources B and C. If B is over utilized it will take more material from resource A than is needed and C will not be able to supply parts to down stream operations. In companies where there is a large amount of diverging operations, misallocation can be a major problem. To prevent a misallocation of material resources B and C should be provided with schedules to tell these operations to produce a certain amount of material of a specific kind and then stop.

Analyzing Product Flow Types

Once an understanding of the impact of specific product flow has been accomplished determining what the primary flow type is for a specific facility will help tremendously on being able to predict the types of problems which should be prevalent and then providing a solution.

A-Plants

The A-Plant is characterized by a large number of converging operations starting with a wide variety of raw material items being assembled in succeeding levels to create a smaller number of end items. Components are usually unique to the end item and the technology used in assembly operations tends to be highly flexible, general purpose equipment. Under traditional management practices the tendency is to misallocate resource time in an attempt to maximize efficiency and utilization figures. Large batches are used to keep the measurements high resulting in a poor component mix and a constant shortage of the right parts in assembly operations. These large batches move in waves throughout the plant causing temporary bottlenecks to wander from resource to resource. Machines may be underutilized one minute and over utilized the next. Since material is constantly out of balance, overtime is used to "catch up" so that shipments can be made on time. The resulting impact on the quality system is disastrous. Large batches will result in an increase in Inventory and a reduction of visibility. Quality will tend to decrease. Because of the poor material availability and constant expediting there is a high amount of pressure exerted to pass marginal material as acceptable to meet scheduled due dates.

In order to deal with these problems, process batch sizes must be changed so that they maximize utilization on the constraint(s) while transfer batches are made as small as possible. The sequencing and timing of individual orders across all operations should be synchronized with the schedule created for the constraint operation(s). Operators and foreman are encouraged to activate resources to produce only what is required. Buffers designed to protect the Throughput of the system from those things which will go wrong, are used for shipping, constraint and assembly operations (see chapter 6).

The typical A-Plant would be a manufacturer of complex make to order products. Figure 3.11 is indicative of the A-Plant product flow structure for one product.

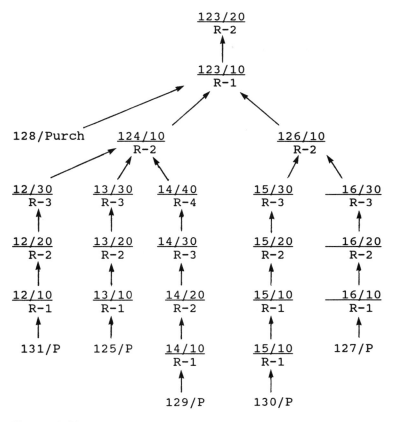

Figure 3.11 A-Plant product flow.

V-Plants

V-Plants are characterized by constantly diverging operations with a small number of raw material items being converted into a large number of end items using highly specialized and expensive equipment. Since each diverging point in the process is an opportunity to misallocate material, the V-Plant, unlike the A-Plant, is dominated by this problem. Under the traditional approach expensive equipment must be utilized constantly to absorb overhead and to insure that adequate value is received. Setups are extensive so batch sizes will be large. Unfortunately, this results in material being taken from diverging operations in quantities larger than required. One leg of the divergence will be unable to perform because the other leg received material which should have gone to it. If material is misallocated prior to the constraint it results in a misutilization of constraint time. Material processed on the constraint which is not dedicated to creating Throughput results in a decline in ROI. Material misallocated after the constraint will result in an increase in finished goods of products for which there is no demand. Customer service levels will be poor. To offset for constantly being out of stock, finished goods inventories will be raised even higher through an attempt to forecast. Like the A-Plant, large batches increase Inventory and reduce visibility while quality suffers. The solution is much the same as that for the A-Plant and that is to synchronize product flows with the systems constraints and customer demand. Lot sizes should be matched to requirements for creating Throughput, while minimizing Inventory and Operating Expense.

The forged products manufacturer would be typical of this type and is represented by figure 3.12.

T-Plants

T-Plants are characterized by a relatively low number of common raw material and component parts optioned into a large number of end items. To support a requirement for meeting short lead time demand a two level master schedule is normally used where common components are schedule and stored just prior to final assembly via forecast and then assembled to order based on specific customer configuration. The T-Plant distinguishes itself from the A-Plant in that the A-Plant is dominated by the convergence interaction, where the T-Plant is dominated by the divergence which occurs just prior to final assembly. Prior to this stage there are no converging or diverging operations. Raw material is processed without being assembled or converted into more than one part, so the number of raw material and sub-assembly components quantities will be the same.

Since diverging operations give opportunity for the misallocation of material, inventories at final assembly will not match customer demand. Customer service

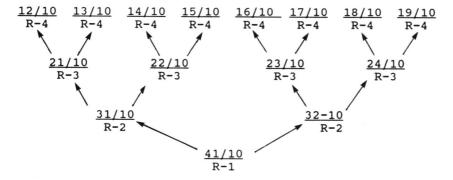

Figure 3.12　V-Plant product flow.

levels will be low. Under traditional management strategies better equipment utilization means larger lot sizes resulting in the same wave effect seen in A-Plants, exacerbating the out of balance conditions in inventories while extending lead times and reducing visibility. Quality suffers. Attempts at "modernizing" the plant and bringing in "new", "more efficient" and "cost effective" equipment may result in less flexibility and an even bigger desire to maximize equipment utilization, making the problem even worse.

T-Plants are best run as two separate facilities; one being make to order and the other being make to stock as in traditional two level master scheduling. However, product flow and demand should be synchronized to the constraint and market demands as in the other plant types, while Inventory or "stock" buffers are placed at final assembly and time buffers are placed at assembly, shipping and constraint operations.

The consumer products manufacturer would be an example of the T-Plant where common components are created using similar processes and then assembled based on the desired customer requirement. Figure 3.13 illustrates the T-Plant.

Combination Plants

Companies do not always fall neatly into the A-, V-, or T-Plant categories. They may have characteristics of each in various combinations. As an example, a forged products facility may be used to feed an assembly plant. This would be an example of a V-Plant feeding an A-Plant. A customized industrial computer manufacturer may purchase raw components for assembly to stock and then final assembly to

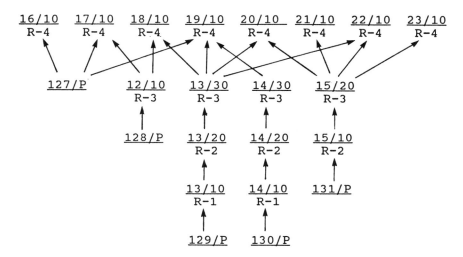

Figure 3.13 T-Plant product flow.

order. This would be an example of an A-Plant feeding a T-Plant.

Once the product flow diagram is complete it gives a detailed record of the relationship of all part/operations and their associated resources to identify characteristics which are inherent to A-, V- or T plants and to understand what instructions are necessary for people who work in specific areas of the production process. As an example, workers in operations just after divergent stations should be aware that a major problem is misallocation and only material required to fulfill the schedule should be taken.

MANUFACTURING SYSTEMS TECHNOLOGY

Finding a physical constraint may be as easy as walking out onto the shop floor and looking for those resources where the inventory is piled up or asking the expediters where they spend most of their time trying to get parts. However, for many companies it is not quite that easy. Trying to identify the constraint or constraints as well as the relationships between resources in a dynamic environment can be very confusing. Erroneous Materials management strategies can cause situations where resource overload conditions physically move from resource to resource without any logical explanation. Many technical paradigms in manufacturing systems technology such as Master Production Scheduling Material Requirements Planning and Capacity Requirements Planning make it virtually impossible to identify physical limitations. It is extremely important that these problems be overcome.

Manufacturing Resource Planning

In most traditional systems the approach to identifying physical limitations statistically begins with the Master Production Schedule (MPS). In creating the MPS an attempt is made to assess the load on all resources at the same time while creating a basic schedule to be input to Material Requirements Planning. Input to the MPS may include sales orders as well as forecasts of end items or spare parts while a load profile representing each product within the MPS is used to determine basic demand requirements for specific resources and time periods. The input to Material Requirements Planning (MRP) in the form of end items and due dates are then used along with current on hand and on order information as well as bill of material information to identify that material required to produce the demand from the MPS. MRP feeds it's output into Capacity Requirements Planning (CRP) in the form of planned releases and due dates so that a detailed capacity report can be produced from routing and resource information. The following figure illustrates.

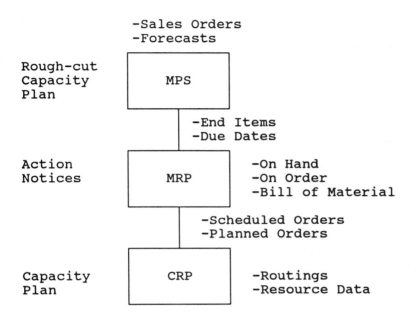

Addressing The Problems

There are three major problems which are fairly consistent throughout the traditional system and seem to violate basic laws governing the impact of product flow and the way in which resources interface. While these three issues do not represent all the problems they are significant.

- Dynamic versus static data.
- The aggregation of demand.
- Interactions between resources.

Dynamic Versus Static Data

The first problem is that data which should be dynamic in nature, such as lead times and lot sizes, are maintained in the item master file as static. The following example is a typical gross to net requirements generation matrix used in creating the material requirements plan. The objective is to illustrate the computations used in generating action notices, for ordering material and for releasing or rescheduling work orders and purchase orders, and for generating input for capacity requirements planning.

Part: AFG	1	2	3	4	5	6	7
Gross Requirements				10			
Scheduled Receipts							
Planned On-Hand							
Net Requirements				10			
Planned Receipts				10			
Planned Releases		10					

Lead Time = 2

Ten AFG parts are required for gross requirements in period four as indicated by output from the MPS. Since there are none on-hand or on-order net requirements are also generated for period four. The net requirement is a signal that a new order must be placed and a planned order generated for period four. This in turn generates a planned release in period two.

The question is, what determined the lead time for the planned release of 10 parts? Lead times are a function of the extent of "Murphy" (those things which will go wrong), of the load which exists on those resources which are at or near full capacity and the size of the transfer batch. So, what produced this arbitrary 2 period lead time? It was generated as an estimate and placed in a file called the item master so that it could be used during the gross to net requirements process. The problem is it has nothing to do with what is happening on the shop floor at the time the capacity estimation is being accomplished. This act serves to inflate inventories which blocked the creation of Throughput and make capacity planning impossible. This was a major problem recognized by JIT. The work around solution was to lower the number of levels in the bill of material so that lead times would not be exaggerated. This meant that all material within certain levels was due at the same time and therefore capacity was again impossible to plan.

The Aggregation of Demand

The second problem is that resource demand is aggregated within time blocks. Capacity is assumed available when in fact it may not be. The traditional method of finding a resource capacity which is constrained is to divide capacity by demand for a given horizon. In this way demand is aggregated over the entire period and is matched to all capacity for the same period. Capacity is considered available at the time an order is to be processed when, in fact, it may not be.

A capacity report may graphically resemble figure 3.14 where the capacity is well below the demand for a given period and yet a capacity limitation could still exist.

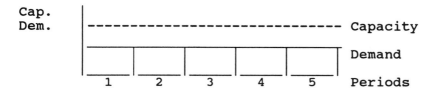

Figure 3.14 Traditional capacity measurement.

In reality, demand for any given day within the schedule may have large peaks and valleys where at one moment there is no demand and in the next moment demand may be twice the available capacity. See figure 3.15.

A certain amount of time is required to protect the delivery of each order to its sales order. To prevent using the protective time and invalidating the sales order, excess demand must be scheduled earlier, not later. Any capacity which exists after the excess demand must be scheduled, in this case to the left, and not aggregated across the entire period.

To determine whether a capacity limitation exists means that the cumulative effect of excess demand must be known for the entire horizon. To do this a schedule must be created which begins at the end of the horizon and schedules excess demand constantly toward time zero allowing for enough protection to insure the sales order can be made on time. There are two issues; that resource which has managed to push the most demand into an earlier time period, and those orders which will appear past time zero. That resource which has the highest amount of load pushed into an earlier time period, allowing for adequate protection to meet the sales order due date and has resulted in pushing the load the farthest past time zero, is the prime candidate for the constraint.

To form a valid schedule means pushing the demand forward into the present on the primary constraint and then determining whether protective capacity is available on the non-constraints so that this new schedule will not be threatened. See figure 3.16.

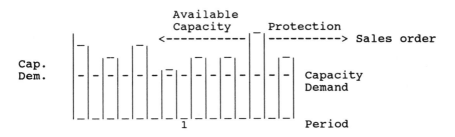

Figure 3.15 The impact of reality on capacity measurement.

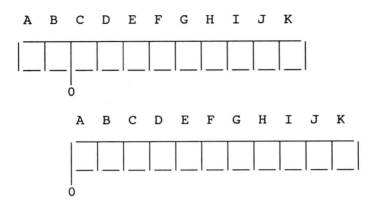

Figure 3.16 Non-traditional adjusting for time zero.

In dealing with the non-constraints the method and problems are somewhat similar except that demand for all other resources must be determined by the schedule created on the primary constraint and not the sales order. Whenever it is discovered that additional resources suffer from the same cumulative effect of a lack of adequate protection it may be necessary to declared them as secondary constraints and a schedule created for them as well, insuring that the time for each is maximized.

Interactions Between Resources

The third problem is that because each resource within a chain of resources will have a direct impact on the schedule produced on the next, constraints can only be located and dealt with one at a time. The following figure illustrates.

```
          A     B
    *----*----*----*
        90%   100%
```

Resource A is a near constraint loaded at 90%. Resource B is the constraint at 100%. In order to exploit resource B so that more Throughput can be generated a schedule which maximizes B's time is generated increasing B's load.

During the scheduling process it may be found that by combining certain orders more Throughput can be generated. Until the outcome of the combination process is known no schedule or load can be determined for any other resource within the chain. They have no idea what the sequence will be to meet B's demand.

The Impact of Data Inaccuracy

While some production operations do not require systems to identify a constraint and create a level schedule, most companies will find that to understand the relationships between primary and secondary resource constraints, a system will be required. Any time computer systems are addressed for managing manufacturing companies, data accuracy becomes a major issue. Fortunately, this issue is less of a problem than originally thought. Data accuracy only becomes an issue when it threatens those resources which have marginal capability to deal with inaccuracies. A resource which is loaded to 100% of its capacity has a much lower tolerance to inaccurate data than does a resource which is scheduled to 20%.

The Introduction of the Diagnostic System

Determining the relationships between resources and their impact on each other is the role of the new diagnostic systems designed for the dependent variable environment and raises some interesting questions:

- What is the impact if a part is scheduled on a resource which has minimum protective capacity and is between the constraint and the delivery of the sales order?

```
-------A---------B-------S/O
    100%        90%
```

- What is the impact if a part is scheduled on a resource which has minimum protective capacity and is between the constraint and the release of raw material?

```
-------A---------B-------S/O
    90%         100%
```

A more detailed explanation of the diagnostic system is addressed in chapter fourteen on Facing The Strategic Issues.

• • •

While understanding the physical environment is critical to supporting a process of "continuous profit improvement", it is extremely important to remember that most constraints will not be physical. They will be created by invalid policies which will surve to inhibit the ability to maximize resource utilization in the creation or protection of Throughput.

• • •

4

Analyzing Policy Constraints

This chapter introduces the concept of policy analysis and provides a method to develop simple solutions.

OBJECTIVES

- To understand the basic concept of policy analysis.
- To present a process for analyzing poor policies.
- To begin to understand how to overcome policy problems associated with the five step improvement process discussed in chapter two so that constraints can be exploited, other resources can be subordinated to them and so that they can be elevated when desired.
- To begin to understand how to create simple solutions.

The Concept Of Policy Analysis

Perhaps the biggest limiting factor to a company's ability to make money are internal policies. Poor policies act as *inhibitors* to interfere with the maximization of Throughput from existing constraints or to falsely assume a necessity of sub-optimization between two supposed absolutes. As an example, a policy of maximizing the utilization of every resource is supposed to maximize profitability, but will ultimately cause bankruptcy by increasing inventories and interfering with a physical resource constraint's ability to create Throughput. EOQ assumes that a sub-optimization must be struck between the cost of setup and the cost of carrying Inventory but setups costs are not a constant. The cost of setup in one work center may impact Throughput while the cost at another may not exist at all.

47

• • •

Because there will always be a constraint to a company's making more money the probability is very high (100%) that at some point in time the company will arrive at a situation where it will not have experience at breaking it.

• • •

To identify and solve these issues takes more than an analysis of the physical environment. While a diagnostics capability is useful in gaining additional insight, it cannot identify non-physical limitations. What is needed is the capability to analyze effects which occur in the environment so that core causes can be discovered and simple solutions developed.

EFFECT-CAUSE-EFFECT

There are numerous tools available which are used regularly to look for core causes. The preferred tool for looking at policy constraints to increasing Throughput is termed Effect-Cause-Effect. Figures 4.1A and 4.1B illustrate.

In using Effect-Cause-Effect certain negative effects are selected and causes are pre-supposed. These pre-supposed causes should have supporting effects. If a sup-

Pre-supposed Causes	Supporting Effects
- New product/markets not established while old markets stagnating	- New product/markets not available - Sales reps concentrating in old markets
- Decision of President to stay in current market	- Unwritten policy - We are a defense contractor
- The perception that costs are too high to compete in the commercial market	- Confirmation from president
- Erroneous decision model	- Confirmation of method used *Cost of Goods Sold* (COGS) - Confirmation of the existence of excess capacity through diagnostics capability

Figure 4.1A   Effect–Cause–Effect (Effect: Slow increase in sales; origin: sales reports).

porting effect is found for the cause, then the probability of a relationship is increased and the cause is assumed to be valid. This chain of events is continued until the core cause is found and is an improvement over normal cause and effect diagrams, such as the fish-bone chart because of the increased probability that the supposed cause is valid.

In this case, a defense contractor's sales were increasing at a slow pace. It was determined that since the old markets were also growing at a slow pace that new markets must be established to expand. Since, in this case, the perception was that price competitiveness prevented them from expanding into the civilian market, the company would simply have to live with slow growth. The core cause was determined to be an invalid cost method using the traditional *cost of goods* sold to determine *costs*. (See Chapter five on Correcting the Decision Process.)

- To create the Effect-Cause-Effect Diagram the following steps are used:
- Identify a negative effect in the environment for which an analysis is to be performed.
- Develop a list of supposed causes and look for supporting effects.
- Enter those supposed causes underneath the primary effect and add the supporting effect to one side.
- Draw an arrow from the supposed cause to the primary cause. Also draw an arrow from the supposed cause to the supporting effect.
- Repeat the process until the core cause has been found.

The key is to locate the core cause and to eliminate it. Once eliminated, all the intervening supporting effects and causes as well as the original negative effect should disappear. If not, then the core cause was not discovered. Often the core problem was created by an erroneous assumption. However, it may not be obvious to everyone that the assumption is incorrect. The assumption may be analyzed through the use of the Assumption Model.

ASSUMPTION MODEL

Proper verbalization of a problem can help to solve major issues like the core problem described below. Whenever difficult decisions are made an *Assumption Model* is used which supports the verbalization of the issues involved and organizes possible solutions. It is usually used in conjunction with Effect-Cause-Effect.

In the model described a company is having constant work stoppage at a resource which is a non-constraint but is loaded to 85% capacity and is threatening the effectiveness of the constraint which it feeds. Based on the Effect-Cause-Effect diagram (figure 4.1B), it seems the core cause is a no hire policy brought about by the Chief Financial Officer wanting to control expenses. A dilemma is caused by a need to protect the constraint and keep expenses low resulting in the need

Pre-supposed Causes	Supporting Effects
Shaft out of Specification	SPC Charts
Lathe out of tolerance	Chart interpretation
Low oil level	Chart interpretation
Lathe not properly serviced	Service records
Maintenance personnel not available	Employee records
No hire policy	Maintenance supervisor
CFO wants to save money	Comments by CFO

Figure 4.1B   Effect–Cause–Effect (Effect: Constant work stoppage at lathe; origin: work reports).

for hiring a new employee and not hiring at the same time. The Dilemma is modeled in figure 4.2. In this model several assumptions have been made which are either valid or invalid. If one of the assumptions can be proven wrong or solved in another way the entire problem will no longer exist. Each participant in the process wants to increase Return on Investment and have taken different routes to attain their goal. Therein lies the problem.

Obviously, the assumption made from B to D can be broken immediately. Increasing capacity can be accomplished in a number of different ways. Since the problem is caused by an intermittent low oil problem one way to solve it would be to have the operator or someone else who has excess capacity add oil to the machine on a regular schedule. Another solution might be to spread the work over

```
                    (B) Increased          (D) Hire
                        Capacity
    (A) Improve ROI

                    (C) Low O/E            (E) NO Hire


                        Assumptions

AB - Must have increased capacity to protect ROI
AC - Must have Low O/E to protect ROI
BD - Must hire to increase capacity.
CE - Must not hire so that O/E stays low.
DE - You cannot Hire and Not Hire at same Time
```

Figure 4.2   The assumption model.

a number of machines reducing the amount of oil consumed. A process change may eliminate the need for the machine altogether.

To create the Assumption Model the following steps are used:

- Determine the goal which must be accomplished and the prerequisites which must occur relative to the problem being addressed. (Positions A, B and C in the diagram above.)
- Determine the prerequisites for positions B and C so that positions D and E can be entered.
- Determine the assumptions being made for each position on the diagram (A-B, A-C, B-D, C-E, and D-E) and right them below the diagram.
- Analyze each assumption for validity or for alternative solutions.
- Develop a list of alternatives for further analysis.

POSITIVE TREES

Whenever deciding on an alternative solution, especially in situations where there is no experience available to predict what the impact will be, a method for systematically reviewing the details of each change on a level by level basis is needed. This is accomplished through the use of the Positive Tree, starting with the alternative change and then predicting the outcome at each level before continuing on to the next level. Figure 4.3 illustrates.

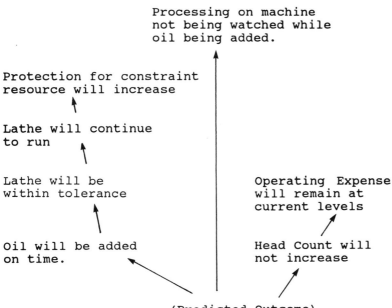

Figure 4.3   The positive tree. Desired change: Operator monitors and adds oil.

In the example shown the desired change is to have the operator do the preventive maintenance procedure of monitoring and adding oil to the machines. The predicted outcome is that oil will be added on time causing the lathe to remain in tolerance so that it will have a greater amount of available time for protecting the constraint. The head count will remain the same so that operating expenses will remain level. A negative effect was discovered in that while the operator is adding oil, the machines will not be watched. This may cause a problem in some resources.

To create the Positive Tree diagram the following steps are used:

- Begin with an alternative problem solution created from the Assumption Model.
- Ask the question "What is the possible outcome or problem which could be created by this solution".
- After establishing an initial outcome continue asking the same question until each branch has been completed.
- Whenever a problem is encountered within a branch, countermeasures for overcoming the problem may be listed out to one side or below. Each countermeasure may be the subject of a separate Positive Tree.
- Select the next problem or possible solution and continue the process.

PREREQUISITE TREE

Once a change has been selected the prerequisites to implementing the change must be known. The Prerequisite Tree is used to systematically identify prerequisites on a level by level basis so that an action plan can be created. Figure 4.4 illustrates.

In the example shown the desired change is to have the operator monitor and add oil. The immediate prerequisite is that the operator would need to be trained and have access to the oil. An action plan can now be developed which would support these prerequisites.

To create the Prerequisite Tree diagram the following steps are used:

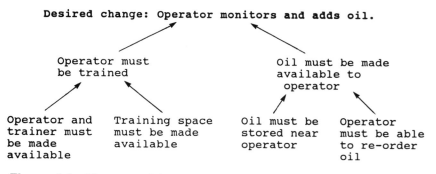

Figure 4.4   The prerequisite tree.

- Begin with the selected problem solution created from the Positive Tree step.
- Ask the question "what is the prerequisite to accomplishing the desired change."
- After establishing the initial outcome continue repeating the question at each level until a complete description of prerequisites has been made.

DEVELOPING THE ACTION PLAN

The Action Plan is used to identify tasks which must be performed and to assign responsibility and a timetable for performance. The Prerequisite Tree identifies the tasks to be performed. Each task is given a time and responsibility based on availability and willingness of people to comply. The Action Plan may also include a list of people who must be trained so that they can invent their own solutions to specific problems. One of the problems encountered in TQM II is overcoming the cost mentality. Having people invent their own solutions has proven to be an invaluable tool.

Task	Resp.	Time
Train operator	Supervisor	1/15/92
Develop procedures for storing oil	Manufacturing Engineer	1/15/92
Develop procedures for ordering oil	Manufacturing Engineer	1/15/92

To create the Action Plan the following steps are used:

- Identify the task to be performed or the concept to be invented from the Prerequisite Tree.
- Select the people who need to accomplish the task or invent the solution.
- For those who must invent the solution, select the proper education which will accomplish the task.
- Select the timetable for the task or education to be completed.

(Note: The limitation of the policy analysis method is that it is only as effective as the knowledge of the person using it. It is a bit understandable that a person experienced in running a production control department may have difficulty applying it to sales.)

• • •

Nowhere is the need for policy analysis more evident than in making decisions.

• • •

5

Correcting the Decision Process

Possibly the greatest impact to any company will come through being able to make consistently valid decisions. In light of discoveries made so far how a decision should be made has radically, but necessarily, changed and will have a major and immediate impact on the profitability of any company. It is the subject of major policy analysis issues.

OBJECTIVES

- To begin to understand what the impact of current decisions are on the profitability of the company.
- To begin the process of understanding how decisions should be made.

• • •

The secret to making good decisions is in being able to predict the impact of the decision on Throughput, Inventory and Operating Expense. It is the environment and the limitations of the system which dictates the solution.

• • •

Not every decision a manufacturer will face could or possibly should be covered in one book. However, insight into how decisions should be made is provided by the following discussion.

QUALITY COST

Whenever Operating Expense is addressed with the intent of improving, one focusing mechanism used is *quality cost*. Conventionally, it is necessary to know the magnitude of the impact of an occurrence in relation to cost. The key indicators are cost and the magnitude or frequency of occurrences. Cost can be related in a multitude of terms; internal failure costs such as scrap and rework, external failure costs such as warranty charges, appraisal costs such as inspection and test, and prevention costs such as process planning and control or education. There can be, quite literally, hundreds and perhaps thousands of these occurrences. So, in an attempt to focus on only the most important issues costs are arranged based on their impact. The *Pareto Analysis* is performed where 80% of the costs are created by 20% of the cost drivers. The problem is that 20% represents a large number and a correction in any one of them results in a very small improvement in profitability. In addition, the mechanisms for analyzing cost information can lead to corrections which have no impact on Operating Expense. Two excellent examples of problems encountered while attempting to use quality cost as a focusing mechanism are rework and scrap.

Rework

In Figure 5.1 there are two resources, "A" and "B". Resource A feeds resource B. Each has a rework cost in the form of additional labor associated with a specific occurrence. For resource A the cost is $10 labor and for resource B it's $20 labor per occurrence. Resource A's frequency rate is 100 per week, resource B's is 200. The total quality costs for rework are $1,000 and $4,000, respectively.

In this way it is very easy to focus efforts. Traditional TQM approaches would require concentrating on the core cause for resource B's problem. It obviously has a greater impact due to the $3000 additional expense. However, in order to review this issue from a global perspective the concept of resource load must be added.

What is the financial impact if the "cost" is labor in a resource which has excess capacity to deal with the additional work? If resource B is loaded to 50% capacity and resource A is loaded to 100% capacity, which is more important to solve? What is the impact of solving a rework problem in resource A or B? This raises some interesting questions which must be answered in order to solve the problem.

- If the problem is solved in resource B will the ability to ship additional product go up, thereby increasing Throughput?

	Cost		Freq		Total Cost
A	$10	x	100	=	$1,000
B	$20	x	200	=	$4,000

Figure 5.1   Computing quality cost.

- Will Operating Expenses be reduced?
- Will Inventory go down?

Figure 5.2 helps to understand the problem a little better.

Resource A feeds resource B so the actual output from resource B is regulated by the capability of A. Resource B has an additional 50% capacity which is going unutilized and can easily overcome any delays in shipping. So, by fixing resource B's rework problem no additional products will be shipped. Throughput would remain level.

The next question is how much will operating expense be reduced? The immediate assumption is that it will be reduced by the amount of the rework cost or $4,000. However, Operating Expense is caused from a global perspective by the salaries which are paid, the rent for the facility and other things such as electricity and insurance. Will any of the cost drivers for operating expense go down? Since the worker is probably being paid for a 40 hour work week and not for work performed, this seems unlikely. Will he be laid of if the problem is fixed? This seems unlikely as well. From a global perspective, the $4,000 savings for fixing resource B is a mirage.

The final question is how much of a decrease in inventory will there be? The question might also be asked whether the delay caused by resource B's rework problem actually resulted in an increase in inventory in the first place. Since resource B exists after the constraint the amount of inventory which would exist between the constraint and the end of the process is regulated by resource A. To result in an increase in inventory a delay in shipment would have to occur. The additional 50% capacity at resource B should insure that due dates are actually met.

To fix resource B would mean that Throughput, Inventory and Operating Expense would remain level. However, if any money is spent trying to solve this problem Operating Expense would go up without a corresponding increase in Throughput, causing profitability to decline.

Now the same questions must be addressed to the global impact of fixing resource A. Since resource A is the governing factor for creating Throughput, and has a limited availability, any increase in A's availability will increase the amount of Throughput being generated. Unless resource A were working overtime Operating Expense would not decline for the same reasons as discussed with resource B. Would inventory decline?

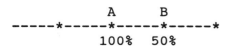

Figure 5.2 The impact of product flow.

Whether or not inventory would increase or decrease depends on the rate of consumption as well as the rate of release of raw material into the system. Increasing capacity on the constraining resource would increase consumption. If the rate of release of material was not increased to keep pace inventory would decline and Throughput would be threatened.

In short, fixing resource A would result in an increase in profit, while fixing resource B would result in no improvement or a possible decline in the bottom line, and yet traditional quality cost approaches would focus on resource B.

Scrap

Figure 5.3 represents two parts, each with a certain scrap ratio, while part B consists of $25 material, $25 labor and $75 overhead. Material is the cost of the raw material it takes to make the part. Labor is the expense of the direct labor expended by factory workers. Overhead represents costs which are not directly related to the labor being expended to produce the part such as engineering expenses or rent for the facility. In traditional accounting these are the basis for creating the standard cost. The profit margin is determined by subtracting the standard cost from the sales price.

Part A is an expensive part which sells for more money and has a greater margin. Part B is a less expensive part. The scrap rates are 20% for part A and 10% for part B. Each part is scrapped at the end of the operation.

Under the quality cost or standard cost system, whenever part A is scrapped the loss is $200 standard cost. Whenever part B is scrapped the loss is $125 standard cost. Obviously, the best decision would be to fix the scrap on part A. It loses more standard cost, has a higher scrap ratio, a higher sales price and a higher profit margin. However, as in the previous example, there are other things to consider. What is the financial impact if part A is being made on resources which have excess capacity? What is the financial impact if part B is being made on resources which are scheduled to 100% capacity. In part A, each time a part is scrapped the loss is the cost of raw material alone. There is excess capacity to replace all but the raw material. In part B, each time a part is lost the entire value of the sales order is lost. It is being made on resources which cannot donate any additional time to make up the difference.

Part	Mat.	Labor	Over Head	Standard Cost	Sales Price	Prof. Margin	Percent Scrap
A	50	50	100	200	300	100	20%
B	25	25	75	125	200	75	10%

Figure 5.3   Computing the impact of scrap.

Sometimes the alternatives are not quite that easy. What would be the impact if the volume of sales for part A were 100 pieces and for part B 40 pieces per month.

```
                          Scrap   total
     QTY    Loss          rate    loss
A    100 x $50   = $5,000 x .20 = $1,000
B     40 x $200  = $8,000 x .10 = $  800
```

In part A the loss is $1,000 per month. In part B the loss is $800 per month, But, with part B because it is being made on resources which are scheduled to 100% capacity and cannot make up any loss, the loss also includes future potential for "sales" by not delivering on time. This may prove to be the biggest problem.

One primary tenet in TQM is that those employees which create an improvement should not suffer layoffs. Regardless of how streamlined the operation becomes, if sales do not go up and Operating Expense is not lowered how can it be said that an improvement has occurred? If increasing the quality of the products and services does not result in an increase in sales and lowering "quality cost" does not result in a decrease in Operating Expense then it must be said that a major problem has been discovered which cannot be ignored. In traditional TQM the focusing mechanisms must be modified.

COST ACCOUNTING

Cost accounting was originally developed around the turn of the century to "judge the impact of a local action on the bottom line". The objective was to assign a value to an occurrence and to judge its impact on the bottom line in the form of cost. It has proved to be inadequate not necessarily because it was not adequate at the time it was developed but because the circumstances of its development have changed considerably. Labor is no longer totally variable. Overhead is a considerably larger portion of cost. The advent of Activity Based Cost (ABC) supports this observation. However, the same basic assumption that the secret to making good decisions is based on cost drivers is counter to reality. Even the creators of ABC are now having second thoughts. Dr. Robert Kaplan from Harvard, one of the chief proponents of ABC, in a May of 1990 National Association of Accountants Global Solutions presentation in Boston, is quoted as stating that ABC cannot be used to make decisions.

ACTIVITY BASED COST ACCOUNTING

The objectives of ABC is to determine what the real "costs of goods sold" are so that a valid product mix can be established for the sales force and to determine

	Mat.	Labor	Over Head	Standard Cost	Sales Price	Profit Margin	Quantity Sold	Thruput Gen.
A	80	60	120	260	300	40	100	22,000
B	80	60	120	260	310	50	200	<u>46,000</u>
								68,000
						Oper.	Exp.	<u>-60,000</u>
						Net	Profit	8,000

Figure 5.4 Applying ABC.

which products are absorbing the most overhead activity so that non-value added activity reduction programs can be properly focused. ABC recognizes that many activities are not related to volume, as in traditional cost accounting, and assumes that activities consume resources and products consume activities. However, when examined from a global perspective ABC has some major flaws in trying to accomplish its objectives.

Applying ABC

Figure 5.4 represents the traditional cost accounting model with some additional features. Two products are shown with specific standard cost information along with the sales price and profit margins for each. Also included are the quantity sold and Throughput being generated by each product. (Remember that Throughput is defined as the sales price minus raw material. In this case it has been multiplied by the quantity sold to determine the total Throughput generated by each part.) Operating Expense is later subtracted to determine the net profit. The quantity sold for each product is the ceiling for the market currently being served.

In this model product A and B have the same standard cost but differing sales prices. Since product B sells for more it is identified as the most profitable product while A is identified as the least profitable. In Activity Based Accounting an attempt is made to re-allocate overhead activities so that "real costs" can be determined. If product B were a new product and therefore absorbed more overhead the cost allocation model might be changed to look like figure 5.5. Part B now absorbs 75% of the overhead allocation for both parts due to the activities of 10 engineers.

	Mat.	Lab.	Ovr. Hd.	Std Cost	Sales Price	Prof. Mar.	Quan. Sold	Thruput Gen.
A	80	60	60	200	300	100	100	22,000
B	80	60	180	320	310	-10	200	<u>46,000</u>
								68,000
								<u>-60,000</u>
								8,000

Figure 5.5 Adjusting for overhead application.

The new overhead allocation model shows that product A is now the most profitable and product B is now unprofitable.

Addressing the Impact

In figure 5.5, notice that while profit margins changed Operating expense as well as the amount of Throughput being generated did not change due to the re-allocation or manipulation of data. This will require that action be taken based on the information presented. So, from a global perspective Net Profit remains the same. The question is, what kind of action will this information create and what will be the impact on the profitability of the company? There are two immediate possibilities:

* The elimination of product B
* The reduction or elimination of non-value added activities associated with B.

In addressing the first issue, what is the impact on the profitability of the corporation if product B is eliminated because it seems unprofitable? If product B is eliminated so will the $46,000 worth of Throughput generated, leaving product A to absorb all Operating Expense for the corporation. Unless Operating Expenses were reduced the resulting net profit would be a minus $38,000 ($22,000 - $60,000).

In any attempt to reduce Operating Expense, it is highly unlikely that the total overhead associated with product B will be eliminated along with the product. If 10 engineers spent 75% of their time working on product B, 7.5 engineers would need to be eliminated. Since this would be physically impossible, short of breaking the law, 3 engineers would probably need to stay to support the A product. Along with the expenses of the engineers, the expenses originating from the rent of the manufacturing facility and the managers and supervisors who work there will probably not be eliminated either. To maintain the same net profit at $8,000, Operating Expenses must drop from $60,000 to $14,000. Few companies can manage a 76% drop in Operating Expense.

Additionally, if the limitation to increasing the cash being generated through sales is that there is no more market available, and if 70% of the engineers will be eliminated, who will design the new products required to be able to increase cash coming into the company?

In addressing the second issue of focusing on eliminating the non-value added activities associated with product B, can an effective program be created which will have a direct impact on the reduction of Operating Expense or the increase of Throughput? Not likely. There are four issues to consider:

* The elimination of non-value added activities may have no direct link to the reduction of Operating Expense.
* At some point the elimination of non-value added activities may threaten those activities which support the generation of Throughput.

- Time spent concentrating on non-value added programs will distract initiatives which may have a greater impact on the profitability of the corporation.
- Reducing non-value overhead activities associated with product B will not result in the Exploitation or Elevation of the constraint (the market in this case) and therefore Throughput will not increase.

Addressing The Seven Wastes

One method for concentrating on the elimination of non-value added activities is eliminating the "seven wastes" of:

- Excess wait time—time the operator spends waiting for a machine to process while he is watching. The thought is that he could be doing something else while waiting.
- Excess transportation—the unnecessary distance a part must travel for any purpose.
- Excess processing—any additional effort used to produce a product.
- Excess Inventory—Inventory not required by down stream operations.
- Excess motion—motion which does not add value to the product.
- Defects—any defective part produced by any operation anywhere in the plant
- Over production—creating products which are not needed by down stream operations

Removing the seven wastes is designed to improve the efficiency of activities associated with specific products. The thought is that if too much overhead activity is being spent on specific products then the increased efficiency of those activities will reduce the amount of time spent and therefor reduce cost. However, a reduction in the seven wastes, unless it is directly linked to the improvement of the constraint(s), may only result in increasing excess capacity available for any specific activity and, with respect to overhead related labor, unless a reduction of the total work force is obtained total Operating Expense will not go down. Even if the people are moved to another operation they are still in the head count of the company and will create operating expense. If Throughput does not go up and or Operating Expense does not go down productivity will not improve.

For a non-value added reduction program which focuses on the "seven wastes" to impact Operating Expense, employees will probably need to be eliminated. A "process of on-going improvement" focusing on the reduction of non-value added activities, which will effectively impact profitability, may mean the constant elimination of employees. What is the strategic impact of this situation? Excess capacity is a strategic weapon to be used to develop new market segments, for growing the company and, if eliminated, can jeopardize overall corporate growth. (See chapter 14 on Facing The Strategic Issues).

```
Routing                      Routing
Part A                       Part B

Res  Op.  Time               Res  Op.  Time
123  10   10                 123  10   10
124  20   30                 124  20   15
125  30   20                 125  30   20


     Time       Demand
Res  Avail.    A      B    Total   Delta
123  7200    1000   2000   3000    +4200
124  5400    3000   3000   6000    - 600
125  7200    2000   4000   6000    +1200
```

Figure 5.6 Internal capacity limitations.

The Impact of Internal Capacity on ABC

Determining the most profitable product mix requires additional information not considered by ABC. In the products described no mention was made of any internal capacity limitations which might exist and yet this is what controls the creation of Throughput coming into the company.

If the amount of capacity is limited for the A and B products due to a specific resource availability a decision must be made to determine the most profitable product mix. See figure 5.6.

Resource 124, due to a lack of available capacity, places a limitation on the total number of As and Bs which can be produced. Under the ABC decision rules, in the example presented, the decision would be to maximize the selling of A over B. If so, the production of 100 As will use 3000 minutes of the available time on resource 124. The remaining 2400 minutes would be left to produce 160 Bs. Figure 5.7 shows the resulting net profit.

```
          Ovr.  Std   Sales  Prof.  Quan.  Thruput
  Mat. Lab. Hd.  Cost  Price  Mar.   Sold   Gen.

A  80   60   60   200   300    100    100    22,000
B  80   60  180   320   310    -10    160    36,800
                                             58,800
                                            -60,000

                                           - 1,200
```

Figure 5.7 The impact of internal capacity on ABC.

While A seems to be the most profitable product under ABC, after reviewing the route file for both products it is discovered that more of part B can be created in less time resulting in more Throughput being generated. If the decision was based on maximizing profitability given current limitations part B would be the most profitable product. Efforts should be made to supply the available market with all 200 B s and then whatever time is remaining should be devoted to making As.

	Mat.	Lab.	Ovr. Hd.	Std Cost	Sales Price	Prof. Mar.	Quan. Sold	Thruput Gen.
A	80	60	60	200	300	100	80	17,600
B	80	60	180	320	310	-10	200	46,000
								63,600
								-60,000
								3,600

The formula for determining the most profitable product mix is cash generated per unit of the limiting resource.

	A		B	
Sales Price	300		310	
Raw Material	80		80	
Cash Generated	220	= $7.3	230	= $15.3
Constraint Time	30		15	

• • •

In the final analysis it is the physical limitations which overshadow any decision process from a global perspective. Neither the profitability of the company, nor the understanding of where to focus improvements could have been predicted by either traditional or Activity Based Accounting.

• • •

PRODUCT MIX

Exploiting the constraint also includes deciding what product mix is the most profitable. Whenever a limitation exists restricting the amount of product which can be produced a decision must be made chosing one product over another so that profits can be maximized.

Figures 5.8 through 5.11 represent a decision process involving the profitability of a company. In figure 5.8 products AFG and DEF have a market potential of 70 and 30 pieces respectively.

AFG is sold for $120 and DEF is sold for $140. There are four resources A, B, C, and D. Each resource has available 2000 minutes during the week. Operat-

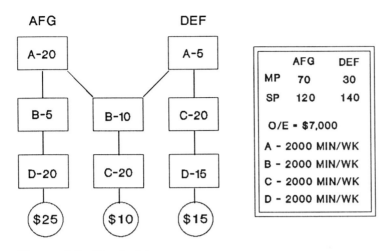

Figure 5.8 The decision process.

ing Expense is $7,000. Bills of material and routings have been combined forming a network of processes beginning with gating operations where raw material enters and proceeding upward until the finished products are complete at the top. Raw material cost is presented in circles. Operations are performed in the amount of time and on the resources indicated in each box. To make part AFG requires $35 raw material be used in the first operation at the bottom on resources D and C. Resource D takes 20 minutes to perform the first operation on the left leg of the net. This operation feeds the next operation to be completed on resource B. The final assembly for AFG takes place at resource A. The middle leg feeds both products. The right leg feeds product DEF. The initial constraint is found to be in resource C. See figure 5.9.

The labor to produce 70 AFGs and 30 DEFs is 2600 minutes. 600 more than the available 2000 minutes per resource.

RESOURCES

PROD.	A	B	C	D
AFG	1400	1050	1400	1400
DEF	150	300	1200	450
TOTAL	1550	1350	2600	1850

Figure 5.9 Identify the constraint.

The Traditional Approach

Because there is a limitation in the amount of time that can be used from resource C, in order to maximize profitability a decision must be made concerning those products which will bring the most amount of profit for the given limitation. Traditionally, the decision process would be based on the concept of profit margin resulting from the formula sales price minus the cost of goods sold. Product DEF is considered the most profitable. It has a sales price of $140 and a raw material cost of $25 while the required labor to produce the part is lower than that required for product AFG. See figure 5.10.

Conventional wisdom would have priority placed on selling all 30 DEFs, creating $3,450 ($140 sales price minus $25 raw material, multiplied by a quantity of 30) in Throughput and using 1200 minutes of resource C's time. Any remaining constraint availability (2000–1200 = 800 minutes) would then be used to make AFGs. Each AFG part takes 20 minutes to produce on resource C resulting in a total of 40 AFGs being made and generating $3,400 ((120–35) × 40) for a total Throughput generation of $6,850. After subtracting $7,000 in operating expense the resulting profit is –$150.

Understanding the Impact of Internal Limitations

The question which should have been asked is not what is the most profitable product, but what is the maximum amount of money which can be made given the limitations of the system? This is determined by the amount of Throughput generated per unit of the constraint. To determine the most profitable product mix,

	AFG	DEF
PRICE	$120	$140
MATERIAL	$35	$25
PROFIT	$ 85	$115
LABOR	75MIN	70MIN

```
Throughput ▪ 30 DEF(140 - 25) ▪   3,450
Throughput ▪ 40 AFG(120 - 35) ▪   3,400
                                   6,850
                        O/E ▪     (7,000)
               NET PROFIT ▪ $  -  150
```

Figure 5.10 Traditional.

considering the limitations provided, the amount of Throughput being generated (sales price minus raw material) is divided by the amount of time used by the limiting resource to create it. In this case the Throughput per unit of the constraint for AFG is $120–35 divided by 20 minutes of constraint time or $4.25 per minute. The Throughput per unit of the constraint for DEF is $140 –25 divided by 40 minutes of constraint time, or $2.88 per minute.

Using the same information but changing the decision process has a much different result. The amount of labor required from the constraint is much less for each unit of the AFG product. The revenue generated per unit of the constraint is higher. See figure 5.11.

When comparing the Throughput per unit of the constraint it becomes obvious that the most profitable decision would be to maximize the creation of product AFG over DEF. Just the opposite of the cost solution. However, the resulting net profit is also greater under this solution.

This has a major impact not only on which products must be pushed into the market but also on how all the other functions within the organization are to perform including purchasing, production, engineering, materials and quality. If the constraint were to be elevated by adding another 2000 minutes to resource C every function within the organization would need to reevaluate its priorities. If resource D becomes the constraint, AFG is no longer the preferred product to sell. The Throughput generated per unit of the constraint (resource D) now favors product DEF. All work schedules become subject to change and any engineering, quality or production emphasis placed on maximizing Throughput is shifted to resource B.

```
Throughput Generated      85
─────────────────────        ■ $4.25
Constraint Time Used      20

Throughput Generated     115
─────────────────────        ■ $2.88
Constraint Time Used      40
```

```
Throughput  ■ 70 AFG(120 - 35) ■ $5,950
Throughput  ■ 15 DEF(140 - 25) ■   1,725
                                   ───────
                                   7,675
                       O/E ■      (7,000)
                NET PROFIT ■  $     675
```

Figure 5.11 Constraint-based.

MAKE/BUY

Any time markets decline and profitability begins to decrease companies invariably will begin looking for ways to reduce cost. One sure way of cost reduction is involved in the make/buy decision. The thought is that if a vendor can make a part cheaper and reduce the overall cost of products the benefit will be carried to the bottom line. The traditional approach to answering this question is the cost method. The standard cost of the item in question is compared to the price to be charged by the vendor. Figure 5.12 represents a cost matrix showing material, labor and overhead for a given part. The standard cost is shown to be $260. The vendors price for the part is $100. The obvious choice is to buy the part from the vendor.

However, if the secret to making valid decisions lies in understanding the impact on Throughput Inventory and Operating Expense this decision will require further analysis. There are two basic situations.

- If a part is currently being made outside the plant by a vendor, what will be the impact if it is now brought inside the facility?
- If a part is currently being made inside the plant, what will be the impact if it is now made at an outside vendor?

Like most cost based decisions the traditional process uses only cost as the primary factor and does not take into consideration internal resource capability and its impact. If a part is being made internally what will be the impact on the ability to protect and create Throughput. There are three conditions which need expanding.

- Those conditions where excess capacity is to be used.
- Those conditions where protective capacity of non-constraint resources is to be used.
- Those conditions where constraint time is to be used.

Using Excess Capacity

In those conditions where the part was to be built on resources which have excess capacity then the actual cost is only the cost of raw material. If the part was made internally, no one would be hired so Operating Expense would not go up. The actual cost of the part being made internally in figure 5.12 would be $80 compared to the vendors $100.

Mat	Lab	Ovr hd	Std Cost	Vendor Price
80	60	120	260	100

Figure 5.12 The make/buy decision.

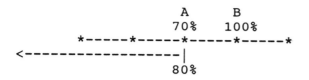

Figure 5.13 The impact of capacity on make/buy.

Using Protective Capacity

If the part were to be made on resources which were marginal in their ability to protect the constraint, adding additional labor demand would reduce the amount of protective capacity available.

Figure 5.13 shows the impact of using protective capacity to produce the part in question. Resource A is a non-constraint which is scheduled at 70% capacity and is feeding the constraint, resource B. Material which was previously obtained from the vendor is now being brought internally and will absorb time from resource A. Resource A's load is now increased from 70% to 80%. This increase in load reduces the probability that A will be able to deliver to B on time. To insure that B is fully loaded there are two choices which must be made. Either material is released earlier resulting in an increase in Inventory and the Operating Expense associated with it or additional Operating Expense will be used in the form of overtime. How much additional Inventory or Operating Expense there will be can only be determined after an analysis of what new limitations would be created. It may result in the creation of a secondary constraint.

If a part were produced internally on resources which were marginally able to protect the constraint, to buy it would mean an increase in the amount of protective capacity available, resulting in Inventory or Operating Expense being reduced. It would also mean an increase in Operating Expense to cover the cost of the product arriving from the vendor.

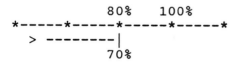

The increase in Operating Expense would be by the amount of the order from the vendor. The reduction could only be determined after physical analysis to determine the impact of the decreased load.

Using Constraint Time

Determining whether a part should or should not absorb constraint time can have several implications.

- Adding more time on the constraint for a particular product will reduce the amount of Throughput generated per unit of the constraint for that product.
- Adding more constraint time for a particular part will impact the amount of time available to produce other products.
- Reducing the amount of constraint time being absorbed by buying parts will increase the amount of Throughput generated but may result in an increase in Operating Expense.
- Increasing the amount of constraint time by making a part will result in a decrease in Operating Expense originating from the vendor but may result in an increase in Operating Expense at the constraint.

Adding demand requirements on constraint resources by making a part internally and increasing the amount of time a particular product absorbs may result in a change in product mix. When comparing Throughput per unit of the constraint to other products a product which had a relatively high ratio may now appear at the other end of the spectrum creating a low Throughput rate and resulting in a change of sales incentive. The following figure 5.14 illustrates.

Product	A	B	C
Sales Price	$100	$150	$200
Raw Material	<u>50</u>	<u>75</u>	<u>100</u>
Throughput Created	$50	$75	$100
Constraint Time-Minutes	15	30	45
Throughput Per Min	3.33	2.50	2.23
Additional Time From New Part	15		
New Throughput Per Min	1.66	2.50	2.23

Figure 5.14 Adjusting the make/buy decision.

Product	Throughput Per Part	Quantity Product Made	Constraint Time Used	Total Throughput
A	$50	50	750 Min.	$2,500
B	$75	50	1500 Min.	$3,750
C	$100	30	1350 Min.	$3,000
			3600 Min.	$9,250

Figure 5.15 Projecting Throughput.

Products A, B and C create $50, $75 and $100, respectively, in Throughput per part and take 15, 30 and 45 minutes to do so resulting in Throughput per minute being $3.33 for product A, $2.50 for product B and $2.23 for product C. An additional 15 minutes is added to product A's time on the constraint changing its Throughput ratio to $1.66 per minute. The impact to product mix was to change product A from the most profitable product to the least.

The impact to other products being run on the constraint cannot be totally known unless a schedule is built which will model the event. However, understanding that in the above case 15 additional minutes per part for product A must be run on the constraint a new product mix and profitability strategy can be created.

Estimating capacity for the constraint at 3600 minutes available time, marketing constraints for products A, B and C at 50 pieces each and using the original labor requirements prior to bringing the previously purchased part inside the plant, the following Throughput projection is made (figure 5.15).

The total Throughput which could be made at this facility is $9,250. After bringing the part in-house from the vendor the following projection is used (figure 5.16).

The impact was the elimination of product A from the product mix in order to maximize profitability and a drop in Throughput generated of $1,100. To increase

Product	Throughput Per Part	Quantity Product Made	Constraint Time Used	Total Throughput
A	$50	0	0 Min.	0
B	$75	50	1500 Min.	$3,750
C	$100	46	2100 Min.	$4,600
			3600 Min.	$8,350

Figure 5.16 Adjusting for the new product load.

the amount of time available and thereby increase Throughput overtime might be required also increasing Operating Expense.

To understand the impact of off-loading product from the constraint to the outside vendor would require a reversal of strategy. Sending the 15 minutes created by product A to the vendor would have increased Throughput from $8,350 to $9,250 but would have resulted in having to pay for the part in operating expense.

Additional Considerations

One consideration not made thus far involves product control. A sensitive part which will impact production to a great extent, if it is poorly made, or if it is unpredictable in it's availability may best be made in-house where it can be better controlled rather than depending on a vendor. Thus it becomes important to study the process of out-sourcing products from all angles, but definitely not from "cost".

PRODUCT PRICING

Product pricing is a key issue in the strategic positioning of any company. While price is usually set by the market the acceptance of any order must include the sellers approval. Price acceptance is usually a function of the predicted profit margin obtained from the algorithm Sales Price minus Cost of Goods Sold. Figure 5.17 represents three possible market segments. The first rectangle is the current market being supported by the XYZ company where product AFG is being sold for $300 and has a standard cost of $260.

Management has been informed by the sales group that two additional markets are available if prices were dropped. In the first market prices must be dropped to $200 and in the second $100. Traditional cost accounting would place the losses for the $200 segment at $60 per part sold and the $100 segment at $160. Most companies would understand immediately that a certain amount of overhead can

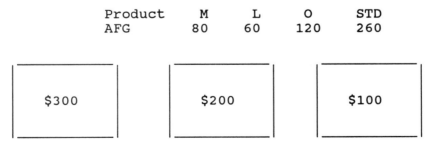

Figure 5.17   Product pricing in segmented markets.

be spread over the new order and so the orders for the $200 market would be grudgingly accepted. Since the price in the $100 market doesn't even cover raw material and labor costs it would be rejected. However, as in the make/buy decision the impact based on a cost matrix is totally unknown. If the parts for the new market segments were to be made on non-constraint resources there would be no additional labor required to handle the new orders. Labor is a non-variable expense in that unless overtime were expended or new people hired payroll will be level at 40 hrs per employee per week at the current head count. The profit for the $200 market is $120 per part and in the $100 market it is $20 per part.

Price Acceptance

In segmented markets, using non-constraint resources, the price should be what ever can be obtained above the price for raw material. As in the make/buy decision any new orders may threaten protective capacity. If a part were made on resources where additional protection would be required it would increase inventories.

If the part were to be made on the constraint, the amount of Throughput per unit of the constraint must be compared to what is currently being produced and, if it is less, then the order should not be taken unless other circumstances dictate. If the $300 and $200 segments were creating an internal constraint it would be very obvious that to take an order from the $100 segment would mean a loss of an order from either of the other two segments.

To properly segment the market:

- The sale of a product in one market segment should not negatively impact the sale of product in another market segment.
- Each market segment must use the same resources.
- The segments should be set so that even though one market is down you will still have adequate business from the other segments.

In order to accept an order the sales representative must know:

- How much each unit of the constraint is being sold for now.
- How much of the constraint will be absorbed by the product in question.
- What the customer is willing to pay.
- Whether the order will impact non-constraints negatively.

LOT SIZING

The determination of proper lot sizes will have a major impact on the overall productivity of the company. If lot sizes are too large, inventories and lead times begin to grow and quality decreases due to a lack of visibility. Products begin competing for sufficient production time on resources with limited capacity, causing

Throughput to be blocked. If lot sizes are too small limited resource capacity is spent supporting setup operations and not production.

The Traditional Approach

The traditional approach was to use the economic order quantity (EOQ) which balanced setup cost with Inventory carrying cost. A larger batch resulted in fewer setups and therefore lower setup cost and higher carrying cost due to an increase in Inventory. A smaller batch resulted in more setups and therefore a higher setup cost but lower Inventory carrying cost.

```
|   .                    *     Carrying Cost
|     .              *
|        .       *
|          .   *
|       *   .
|     *              .      .   Setup Cost
|  *
| *
|_____
```

This approach looks great on paper but immediately falls apart in reality. First, it assumes that the setup cost for all resources is the same. However, a resource which has excess capacity will incur no additional expense unless additional set-ups cause protective capacity to be used. Increased setups on those resources with limited capacity will threaten the creation of Throughput. Increased setups on the primary constraint will cause Throughput to decline immediately. Second, it assumes that the primary costs associated with increased lot sizes are an increase in overhead costs such as interest rates, material handling, storage and insurance while the largest problems are in the restrictive impact on the creation of Throughput. Third, it assumes that the batch size will always remain the same throughout the production process. However, the size of the process batch and transfer batch may be very different. A group technology cell may process in batches of 100, but it will transfer between machines in a quantity of one.

In JIT the optimum lot size has been described as the quantity of one. The reasons given most often for this are:

- To increase visibility.
- To better synchronize production with market demands.
- To increase quality.
- To increase flexibility.
- To decrease lead time.

While these are worthwhile attributes for any manufacturing facility, unless a total perspective is gained through a review of the impact of any lot sizing policy based on Throughput, Inventory and Operating Expense there will be a misinterpretation of the requirements. It must be understood that because the manufacturing environment is dynamic, lot sizes are dynamic as well. In other words there is no optimum lot size for all situations, there are only the impacts certain lot sizes will have given the current situation with respect to capacity availability. So, to determine what the correct lot size is means to determine what the relationships are between the resources the lot is to be processed on at the time it is to be processed. This issue can be easily observed when reviewing the impact of setup savings on resources.

The Impact of Setup Savings

In setup savings the objective is to combine two orders so that one setup can be split between them, thereby maximizing the amount of production time available.

In figure 5.18, to maximize the availability of production time on a constraint resource, product D was pushed up in the schedule so that products A and D could be processed together. As a result, products B and C were pushed out and the total production time increased by the amount of setup saved.

Maximizing production time on a non-constraint operation is usually a waste of time. The only impact may be to increase excess capacity as seen in chapter three on setup reduction. But, on a constraint resource, like setup reduction, setup savings has a positive impact on the amount of Throughput created. This is easy to visualize. However, maximizing production on the constraining resource may have a negative effect on those resources which are loaded to near constraint levels.

In Figure 5.19 resource A is a non-constraint resource, but is loaded to 80% capacity and feeds resource B which is loaded to 100% and is the primary constraint. Resource B's production time and setup time are 80% and 20% respectively. Setup savings is performed increasing the amount of production performed on resource B.

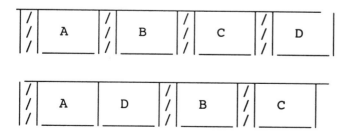

Figure 5.18 Setup savings.

```
              A      B                    Prod S/U
             80%    100%       Before      80   20
     *------*------*------*------*
     <------------- 90%          After      90   10
```

Figure 5.19   The impact of setup savings on near constraint resources prior to the constraint.

If setup savings is performed and production is maximized on resource B, unless the amount of setup savings has the same productive impact on A the load on resource A will increase. The laws governing probability and statistical fluctuation will begin to effect A's ability to deliver to B, threatening Throughput. To offset, material is released earlier causing Inventory to increase. There is a limit to the impact earlier releases will have. Parts cannot be released earlier than time zero. So, to offset for an inability to protect the constraint, overtime will be spent driving Operating Expense upward.

These same problems will occur for resources which have operations which follow the constraint. Figure 5.20 illustrates that when the productive capacity of the constraint is increased, protective capacity on the non-constraints that follow the constraint is decreased. If the impact is severe enough, sales order delivery is threatened.

Notice that in figure 5.20, orders B and C were pushed out. This will result in lowering the amount of protection available for insuring that the sales order is shipped on time. Unless the amount of protective capacity is known on the resources between the constraint and shipping the impact on Throughput, Inventory and Operating Expense cannot be known.

The Small Lot Strategy

The objective of the small lot size strategy is to increase visibility by allowing each part to be observed shortly after production and to decrease lead times. In reducing the lot size while greater visibility is created, more time is used in setting up

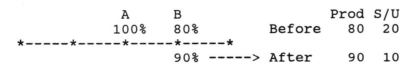

Figure 5.20   The impact of setup savings on near constraint resources after the constraint.

an operation. If the resource on which the small lot is used is a constraint then Throughput will go down due to a decrease in production time available. Unless the impact of setups can be eliminated through a setup reduction program the loss can be substantial. However, setups produce side effects creating disruptions in the flow of products and increasing the opportunity for error.

Conclusion

The large batch maximizes the utilization of a given machine but extends lead times, and increases inventories. The small batch increases visibility, decreases lead times but lowers the amount production on constraining resources by increasing the amount of setups required. The ideal situation would support the desired characteristics of the large and small batch together but be subject to modification based on the dynamics of the current environment. Lead time and visibility are greatly enhanced by using a transfer batch of one. While productivity on constraint and near-constraint resources is enhanced using large production batches.

The size of the production batch can only be determined after a load is placed on all resources for the given schedule and its impact on those resources which have a marginal capability to produce is determined. As a rule of thumb, the best process batch size to start with is the actual customer demand. Adjustments can be made upward by combining customer requirements, if necessary, to maximize Throughput. Transfer batches should be made as small as possible to keep lead times low and visibility high. The end result will be to maximize Throughput while at the same time keeping Inventory and Operating Expenses low.

COST JUSTIFICATION

The traditional justification for an improvement is usually based on the amount of labor saved per unit of product being produced times the labor rate times the number of parts to be produced. However, when reviewed from a global perspective this method begins to fall apart. In figure 5.21, as part of a cycle time reduction program, an engineer offers an improvement to resource B on the left leg of the net by cutting the amount of required labor by 50% at a cost of $3,000 for a fixture.

The productivity model lends some insight into what is important.

$$\text{Productivity} = \frac{\text{Throughput}}{\text{Operating Expense}}$$

Resource B, being a non-constraint resource, does not control the creation of Throughput. It already has excess capacity. When the $3,000 is spent no additional

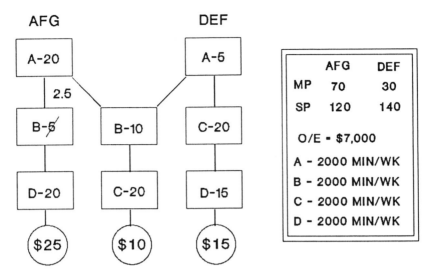

Figure 5.21   Cost justification—the decision process.

money will be coming into the company. Since reducing the amount of labor required will not erase the need for resource B, payroll will not be reduced. Operating Expense went up by the $3,000, while Throughput remained level forcing
productivity to decline. If the $3,000 had been spent reducing the amount of la-
bor required in resource C then the amount of product being produced would increase along with the Throughput being generated. Operating Expense would have
gone up, but, so would Throughput. The key issue now is whether the Throughput being generated will pay for the investment in less time than another option.

Cost justification does not always lead to the intended results. A more effective method would be to Throughput justify.

GLOBAL VERSUS LOCAL MEASUREMENTS

In each of the decision processes given the attempt to arrive at a logical conclusion is made from a local perspective. However, when viewed from a global perspective (Throughput, Inventory and Operating Expense) the traditional decision
processes cease to make sense. Before any real long term improvement can be
attempted these issues must be addressed.

Many companies spend enormous resources trying to reduce cost of goods sold
only to find that Throughput did not go up and Inventory as well as Operating
Expense did not go down. If this does not occur improvement in profits has not
been made.

6

Beyond Just-In-Time

This chapter introduces a superior method for factory scheduling/management which embraces more readily the way in which resources interface and produces a more effective improvement process—the Drum-Buffer-Rope (DBR) process.

OBJECTIVES

- To understand how to create the drum for maximizing constraint utilization.
- To understand what data is required and how it should be manipulated.
- To understand how to create and implement a more effective improvement process which has a direct link to the absolute measurements.
- To understand how the factory schedule is an integral part of the five step improvement process.

THE TOYOTA KANBAN SYSTEM

The Kanban system starts with the customer and extends through the production facility to the vendor. Its objective is to control the level of inventories, reduce lead times and synchronize the factory as well as vendors with the market. It has been called a *pull system* because demands are pulled from down stream operations based on customer requirements. Resources are synchronized through the use of permission slips called kanban or cards. In the two card system depicted in Figure 6.1, there are two types of cards—the production and the move. Material cannot be produced or moved unless a card is available granting permission. Material which has been converted or is to be converted is stored in the outbound or inbound side in containers of small lots. Whenever the succeeding operation has a demand placed on it requiring that parts be taken from the outbound side of the process, as the material is being carried away, the production card which was at-

INBOUND   OUTBOUND

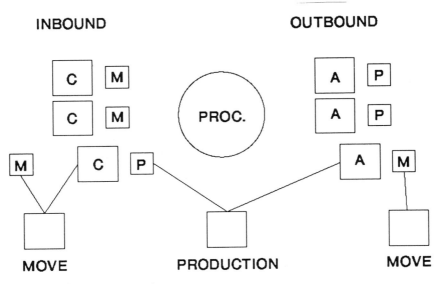

Figure 6.1   The two card system.

tached is removed and used to secure parts from the inbound side so that replace-ment cards can be made. Notice the outbound side of the process where the A parts are being moved using the M card and the P card is used to obtain the C parts for processing. Unless the operator has a P card he cannot begin production. He will remain idle. Inventories are not allowed to build as in traditional manufactur-ing. Lot sizes remain low which keeps lead times low as well.

In the one card system, the inbound and outbound sides of resources are com-bined so resources share inventory locations. Since material does not require a separate movement system, the move cards are eliminated and only the produc-tion cards are used. In a cardless system, action is taken simply by the absence or presence of material as a signal. No cards are used. (See Japan Management Associates, 1986).

For the repetitive manufacturer, just-in-time has created a major opportunity for reducing lead times and increasing productivity. However, there are some major problems which must be overcome.

Lack of Flexibility

Just-in-time lacks the flexibility required by most manufacturers and therefore its applicability is limited to the repetitive environment. In the one or two card sys-tem, Inventory is stored in the kanban squares at the container amount to be used as buffers between operations and to shorten the time and distance traveled to and from the stock room to find replacement parts for those used. Since the predict-ability of configuration is much lower for the job shop environment than for the repetitive manufacturer, a much larger Inventory must be maintained between operations for replenishing a larger number of configurations, making this alternative too expensive. Some manufacturers have combined MRP with JIT to provide the flexibility needed (Synchronous MRP), but the result has not met expectations. Inventory as well as kanban must be replaced in the kanban square with material for the new configurations on a regular basis and the old material stored, producing a logistical nightmare, especially for large facilities.

Vulnerability

Since each resource is dependent on the succeeding resources for production signals, whenever there is a disruption in the flow due to quality, a lack of materials or problems in setup, the entire line is shut down. Operations which exist prior to any disruption will cease to get production signals from downstream operations, while operations which appear after any disruption will be starved for parts.

Creates Additional Inventory

Kanban, while it has been touted as a pull system in synchronizing the shop floor is actually a push system which creates more Inventory than is needed. It pushes Inventory into the kanban square whether it is actually required or not. Just because a part is removed from the outbound side does not mean it needs to be replaced.

Improvement Process is Disruptive and Lacks Focus

To create an improvement in JIT, one method is to remove Inventory from kanban squares until a resource is unable to fill the succeeding resources demand in a sufficient amount of time causing disruptions to occur in the production process. The disruptions are fixed by decreasing the amount of time required to replace the Inventory. This reactive method causes the output of the facility to decline immediately and may not result in an overall increase in Throughput after the disruption has been repaired because the total long term output of the facility may be governed by a different resource but, due to a specific product mix or short term problem the disruption occurred elsewhere in the system.

Those improvements which are focused on the reduction of waste at and between all operations as measured by cycle time may have an impact on the reduction of Inventory, but will not have an impact on the overall output of a manufacturing facility until those resources which have limited ability to produce are improved.

Finally, Just-in-time represents a poor implementation of the five step improvement process. If the objective is to maximize the output of a facility, that resource which has the greatest limitation must govern the way in which the factory is scheduled and not the market. The creation of the schedule at the constraint represents a portion of the exploitation phase and may include efforts to maximize the constraints ability to produce Throughput thereby invalidating the schedule established by the market. The trick is to accomplish the reschedule in such a way that sales orders are not late. JIT avoids this issue.

Long Implementation

The implementation of JIT is a long term and complex endeavor. It requires a more sophisticated and better trained work force than is generally found. The small lot size strategies require that vendor, setup reduction and quality programs be very successful to prevent drastic fluctuations in output. Typical implementations run in the several years time frame requiring a tremendous commitment in time, resources and money over a long period.

THE DRUM-BUFFER-ROPE METHODOLOGY

The Drum-Buffer-Rope (DBR) methodology is a technique for developing a smooth, obtainable schedule for the plant and for maximizing and managing the productivity of a manufacturing facility from a global, not a local, perspective (Umble and Srikanth, 1990). It differs from other manufacturing techniques in that it concentrates on determining the relationships between resources in resolving conflicts to creating a smooth flow of product and is applicable to all types of processes whether they are repetitive, process or job shop. DBR also provides an improved method of focusing protection so that the impact of disturbances in smooth product flow can be minimized.

• • •

However, the DBR process was designed as an implementation of the exploitation and subordination steps in the five step process of *continuous profit improvement* and therefore represents a tremendous leap forward in managing the shop floor from a profitability perspective. It distinguishes itself in that it represents how a factory should be scheduled based on what has been learned so far in this text rather than presenting just another alternative.

• • •

The Drum

The drum is the schedule for the systems constraint and represents a portion of the exploitation phase of the five step improvement process. It is used to maximize the available time of the constraint and to create the Master Production Schedule

(MPS). Like the base drum in a marching band, it is the drum beat of the manufacturing facility. All other resources produce in synchronization to the constraint's schedule.

In order to schedule the constraint an attempt is made to place the start and stop times for each order on a time line so that two conditions are met:

- Enough protection is available to insure that each sales order due date is met.
- No conflicts exist between orders attempting to occupy the same space at the same time.

While the second condition must be met to create a valid schedule, obviously, the first condition is subject to the results of the second. If time is not available sales orders will be pushed out and due dates invalidated.

Additional considerations arise when secondary constraints begin to appear. These are resources which have been scheduled to near capacity levels and because of this issue will have trouble meeting the demands of the primary constraint schedule. After the primary constraint has been scheduled, resources which are loaded to near constraint levels must be protected to insure that the schedule for the primary constraint can be met. Secondary constraint schedules must be built so that whatever time is available on the secondary constraints can be maximized. However, building the secondary constraint schedule must consider the schedule already established for the constraint. So, when building the secondary constraint, an additional consideration must be added. There must be no conflicts between the primary and secondary constraint schedules.

Since the primary schedule has been set the secondary schedule must attempt to schedule around it. If unsuccessful, a reschedule of the primary constraint must take place.

The Buffer

The buffer is a time mechanism used to offset for those things which will go wrong and determines the lead time for products from the gating operations. The buffer is equal to the processing time plus the setup time plus an estimate of the aggregated amount of protective time required to insure that the product will get to the *buffer origin* when needed. There are 3 areas (buffer origins) which need protection:

- Shipping to insure parts are delivered to the customer on time.
- The constraint to insure maximum utilization of constraining resource time.
- Those assembly operations in which one leg of the process is fed by a constraint and the other is fed by non-constraints so that parts which were processed on the constraint will not wait in the assembly operation before parts from other non-constrained resources arrive.

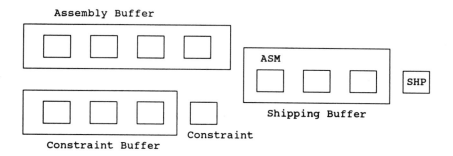

Rope

The rope is the synchronization mechanism for the other resources and consists of the release schedule for all gating operations. Technically the rope is equal to the constraint schedule date minus the buffer time. The release of material determines the timing for parts being processed on the non-constraint resources.

APPLYING DRUM-BUFFER-ROPE

Establishing the Data Base

Figure 6.2 contains the sales order, product flow, inventory and resource data information used to compute the placement of orders. The sales order and resource information is self explanatory. However, the product flow, inventory and resource data information referred to as the Net will need some discussion. The top blocks in the Net represent the two products listed in the sales order file, AFG and XYZ. The larger, segmented blocks represent each part/operation or station, the resource, and the amount of time required to process each part (similar to the product flow diagram discussed in chapter three). In the diagram shown the first large block appearing at the top of the structure and high-lited in bold print is an assembly operation for part AFG, operation 10. It is shown as AFG/10 and takes ten minutes to process on resource A. Processing time appears just to the right of the resource information and above the part/operation. Part/operation ABC/10 appearing at the bottom of the left leg of product XYZ and also high-lited in bold print has 10 pieces of Inventory finished at that location and ready for processing at operation ABC/20. Inventory appears just outside and to the right of the block. The setup time is shown in the resource data appearing below the Net information.

Developing the Drum

Placing Orders on the Time Line

The first step in placing orders on a time line for creating the drum is to insure that adequate protection exists between the sales order due date and the time an

Sales Order	Part	Quantity	Due Date
S/O123	AFG	20	154
S/O124	XYZ	10	154
S/O125	AFG	20	155
S/O126	AFG	20	155

The Net

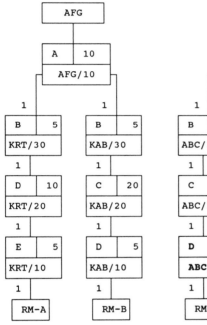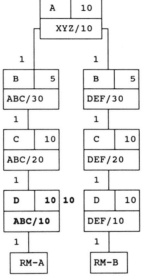

Resource Data

Resource	Capacity	Setup	Quantity
A	960	15	1
B	480	30	1
C	480	15	1
D	480	10	1
E	480	15	1

Buffer Data

Type	Length
Shipping	16 hours
Constraint	8 hours
Assembly	9 hours

Figure 6.2 The DBR data base

order is due to be completed on the constraint. To protect the ship date and to determine the approximate time an order must cross the constraint, the shipping buffer is used. The initial placement of an order will be equal to the sales order due date and time minus the amount of the buffer (aggregation of murphy).

Resource C has been tentatively identified as having the largest load, so developing the schedule will begin there.

- Each sales order is assumed due at the last hour of each 8 hour working day.
- The shipping buffer is estimated at 16 hours or 2 days.
- To place each order on the time line for resource C each sales order due date is used to begin the processing.
- Current bill of material relationships and available Inventory above the constraint are established so that the load can be determined for each order crossing the constraint.

The downward processing through the product structure begins with the farthest out sales order in the horizon -sales order S/O126, for product AFG, quantity 20 and due on shop date 155. Since the schedule being created at this time is for resource C, only those part/operations processed on resource C need to be considered.

Determining the Load

To determine the total demand of resource C's time created by S/O126 the total processing time for each part/operation is multiplied times the quantity required. Since there is no inventory available and since there is a one to one relationship between levels in the product structure, S/O126 will create demand for 20 pieces of KAB/20 at 20 minutes per piece, or 400 minutes. The 30 minute setup time requirement for the C resource is added for a total of 430 minutes.

Determining the Completion Time

The initial placement of orders is determined by subtracting the buffer time from the sales order due date and time. The completion time for KAB/20 S/O126 is set day 155 hour 8:00 (155/8:00) minus the 16 hour shipping buffer or day 153 hour 8:00 (153/8:00).

Determining the Start Time

The start time for the order is set for 153/8:00 minus 430 minutes or 153/0:50.

Completing the Initial Placement

The 430 minutes required for S/O125 part/operation KAB20 is also placed at 153/8:00. Each sales order is processed so that all part/operations which cross the constraint are placed. The following figure shows the load placement for days 152 and 153 on resource C.

Sales Order	Ord. Due	Part/ Oper.	Proc. Qty.	Setup Time	Proc. Time	Start Time	End Time
S/O123	154	KAB/20	20	30	400	152/0:50	152/8:00
S/O124	154	ABC/20	10	30	100	152/5:50	152/8:00
S/O124	154	DEF/20	10	30	100	152/5:50	152/8:00
S/O125	155	KAB/20	20	30	400	153/0:50	153/8:00
S/O126	155	KAB/20	20	30	400	153/0:50	153/8:00

Figure 6.3 is a graphic representation.

Leveling the Load

Obviously, the load must be leveled and sense the protection has been placed to the right, the only direction to level the load is to the left. To create a level schedule, orders must be leveled beginning with the end of the horizon and the start date and times must be placed end to end. Figure 6.4 illustrates.

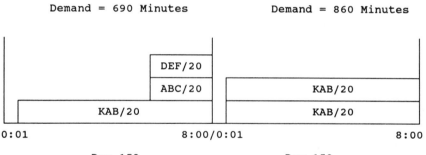

Capacity = 480 minutes

Demand = 690 Minutes   Demand = 860 Minutes

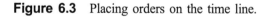

Figure 6.3 Placing orders on the time line.

Sales Order	Ord. Due	Part/ Oper.	Proc. Qty.	I N	Setup Time	Proc. Time	Start Time	End Time
S/O123	154	KAB/20	20		30	400	150/6:06	151/5:16
S/O124	154	ABC/20	10	10	30	100	151/5:17	151/7:27
S/O124	154	DEF/20	10		30	100	151/7:28	152/1:38
S/O125	155	KAB/20	20		30	400	152/1:39	153/0:49
S/O126	155	KAB/20	20		30	400	153/0:50	153/8:00

Figure 6.4 Leveling the load.

The first part/operation to be placed is KAB/20 for sales order S/O126. Its ending time is placed at hour 8:00, day 155 minus the 16 hour buffer or 153/8:00. Its start time is 153/8:00 minus the 430 minute setup and processing time or 153/0:50. Part/operation KAB/20 for S/O125 ends at 153/0:49 and begins at 152/1:39. This process continues until all orders have been placed on the time line for resource C.

Insuring Constraint Utilization

Notice that Part/operation KAB/20 for S/O123 has no Inventory available to begin processing. Since this situation will immediately invalidate the schedule, a decision must be made to process those part/operations which have available Inventory. Since ABC/20 for S/O124 has Inventory, it will be processed first.

Sales Order	Ord. Due	Part/ Oper.	Proc. Qty.	I N	Setup Time	Proc. Time	Start Time	End Time
S/O124	154	ABC/20	10	10	30	100	150/6:06	151/0:16
S/O123	154	KAB/20	20		30	400	151/0:17	151/7:27
S/O124	154	DEF/20	10		30	100	151/7:28	152/1:38
S/O125	155	KAB/20	20		30	400	152/1:39	153/0:49
S/O126	155	KAB/20	20		30	400	153/0:50	153/8:00

The time from 150/6:06 until 151/0:16 should be spent processing Inventory which feeds the constraint based on the constraint's new schedule so that it does not run out of material. It should be noted that in DBR material is allocated based on first come first serve while the schedule for the constraint is based on a finite set back methodology.

Graphically, the new schedule looks like figure 6.5.

Re-scheduling for time Zero

Notice that in the graphical schedule time zero appears at the beginning of day 151. This means that the time available for day 150 does not actually exist, it occurred

Part/Operations

ABC20	KAB20	DEF20	KAB20	KAB20
150	151	152		153

Date/Time

Figure 6.5   Insuring constraint utilization.

Sales Order	Ord. Due	Part/ Oper.	Proc. Qty.	I N	Setup Time	Proc. Time	Start Time	End Time
S/O124	154	ABC/20	10	10	30	100	151/0:00	151/2:10
S/O123	154	KAB/20	20		30	400	151/2:11	152/1:21
S/O124	154	DEF/20	10		30	100	152/1:22	152/3:32
S/O125	155	KAB/20	20		30	400	152/3:33	153/2:43
S/O126	155	KAB/20	20		30	400	153/2:44	154/1:54

Figure 6.6   Rescheduling for time zero.

yesterday, so a reschedule must take place pushing out the schedule of each order by the amount of time scheduled into day 150. Part/operation ABC/20's schedule has been placed 114 minutes into day 150. To reschedule, part/operation ABC/20 for S/O124 must be placed at time zero on day 151 and a schedule created, processing from the earliest time to the latest. Figure 6.6 shows the new schedule.

Notice that the original protection of 16 hours allotted for insuring that orders arrive at shipping on time has been maintained for all but one order. Part/operation KAB/20 for S/O126 now has a scheduled completion date of 1 hours and 54 minutes past the 16 hour buffer. Since this is less than 50% of the total protection allowed, ordinarily, it should not be a problem. The schedule is considered to be on time.

If there were a problem where the scheduled completion date were over 50% of the buffer time, something would need to be done to gain more output from resource C such as setup savings, overtime or off loading onto another resource. If unsuccessful, a reschedule of the sales order may be required.

Developing the Rope

So far what has been accomplished is the schedule for the constraint. However, each operation must be synchronized to the demands of the constraint or to the sales orders. The release schedules for raw materials into gating operations serves as the synchronizing mechanism.

- In developing the rope the release dates of raw materials into gating operations are also determined by the amount of protection necessary.
- For those items which go through the constraint, the drum schedule minus the constraint buffer equals the release date.
- For those items which do not go through the constraint, the sales order due date minus the shipping buffer is used.
- Whenever a part does not go through the constraint, but is used to assemble with parts that do, the assembly buffer designates the release date.

Raw Mat.	Quantity	Release Date
RM-B	20	151/0:00
RM-B	10	151/1:22
RM-B	20	151/3:33
RM-A	20	151/7:00
RM-B	20	152/2:44
RM-A	40	152/7:00

Figure 6.7 Developing the release schedule.

Figure 6.7 illustrates the release schedule and raw material demand to meet resource C's requirements from the above schedule.

Protecting the Constraint

In figure 6.6 part/operation KAB/20 for S/O126 for a quantity of 20 is scheduled across the constraint at 153/2:44. The amount of protection required for the constraint is 8 hours resulting in a raw material requirement for RM-B of 20 parts due at 152/2:44.

Offsetting for Assembly Buffer Requirements

Demand for 20 RM-As is also created by S/O126 and is used in the non-constrained leg feeding the assembly operation AFG/10. Its timing is set for 155/8:00 minus 16 hours shipping buffer minus 9 hours assembly buffer, placing the release time at 152/7:00. Demand of RM-A for S/O125 is due also on 152/7:00 and has been combined with S/O126's RM-A demand. RM-B required on KAB/20 for S/O123 is due at 151/2:11 minus 8 hours or 150/2:11. Since this is past time zero the time is moved to 151/0:00.

Dynamic Buffering

Dynamic buffering is a method used to improve the buffering process so that overall buffer sizes can be shrunk, decreasing Inventory, and only the times when non-constraint resource protective capacity is threatened, will an increase in buffer size and the resulting earlier release date of raw material be considered. There are two conditions. Figure 6.8 illustrates.

```
                    90%         100%
A           *----*----*----*----*

                    100%         90%
B           *----*----*----*----*
```

Figure 6.8 Adjusting for near-constraint resources.

In example A, a resource which exists between the constraint and the release of material has been loaded to 90% as a result of the constraints schedule, limiting the amount of protective capacity necessary. The same condition exists in example B. However, the resource with limited protective capacity exists between the constraint and the sales order. These are the conditions under which an increase in the amount of protection that is necessary will result in an earlier release of material or a reschedule of the sales order so that additional capacity can be found and is the purpose of dynamic buffering.

A comparison must be made between the amount of capacity available and the demand placed on each non-constraint resource being utilized by part/operations which exist before and after the constraint schedule.

FOCUSING ON INVENTORY

Establishing the Basis

Throughput exists to create wealth. It is the mechanism by which money enters the company. Inventory and Operating Expense exists to cause the Throughput figure to be generated and to also protect it. Once a rate of generating Throughput has been established for the weak links in the organization only then can the necessary level of Inventory and Operating Expense be determined.

Reducing Inventory requires that the blockers to reduction be identified. However, the objective is not just to reduce Inventory but to also protect the creation of Throughput. Throughput is created at the time of sale so what must be protected is the delivery of the product to shipping. Those resources which have been loaded to the extent that they threaten the delivery of product to shipping must also be protected. Inventory is used to protect these deliveries. So the issue becomes not what is blocking the reduction of Inventory but what is blocking the reduction of protective Inventory. There are two issues:

- The amount of capacity on the non-constraints resources available to overcome those things which are going wrong.
- The individual incidences occurring which increase the amount of protection necessary.

In figure 6.9 resource B is loaded to 100% and if something goes wrong it will result in an immediate loss of Throughput. Resource A is loaded to 80%, and, if

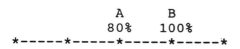
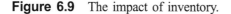

Figure 6.9 The impact of inventory.

something goes wrong, sometimes it will not effect Throughput and sometimes it will by not delivering to B on time.

To solve resource A's problem additional capacity is necessary to protect Throughput.

There are three ways of gaining additional capacity:

- Reduce the number of occurrences which use up the available protective capacity.
- Obtain more of resource A from outside the company.
- Release material earlier so that the demand is spread over more available capacity.

Releasing materials earlier results in raising inventories. To reduce inventories it will be necessary to increase the amount of protective capacity available by eliminating occurrences which use protective capacity.

A prerequisite to reducing Inventory is to first understand when something was supposed to arrive at those areas which are to be protected and whether or not it has arrived. Knowing why something is late will begin to focus attention on those things which are blocking the on time arrival. However, looking for something which is already late is not enough. What is really needed is to understand those actions which are threatening to make something late as it is occurring. The secret to this is to look in front of the time something is supposed to arrive.

Buffer Management

Buffer management is a technique used to manage the amount of protection necessary and to focus improvements on those areas threatening the creation of Throughput and reducing the amount of protection required. An estimate of the amount of protection needed is used to determine the release date of material from the gating operation.

In figure 6.10 a schedule for the constraint resource was developed and a release date was determined after estimating the amount of protection necessary at six hours. This time includes the time required to process the parts on each resource from the gating operation to the protected resource and the amount of time needed to guarantee that, most of the time, the parts will be delivered on time. In this case a specific order was scheduled to begin production on the protected resource or "buffer origin" by 8:00. A 6 hour buffer required that parts be released at the gating operation at 2:00 in order to reach the protected resource by 8:00 so that a specific sales order could be filled on time.

```
Gating            Estimated Protection          Protected
Operation   2:00 |--------------------| 8:00   Resource
```

Figure 6.10 Estimating protection.

The closer to the 8:00 deadline without the arrival of the material, the more threatened the buffer origin becomes. What is needed is a signal to designate when it would be time to find out what is wrong and to expedite so that Throughput would not be jeopardized. In Buffer Management the amount of time given to produce the product is divided into three equal time periods or zones. Zone one is called the expedite zone. If the order does not arrive at the "buffer origin" before the beginning of zone one it is to be expedited. Zone two is the tracking zone. If the order has not arrived before the beginning of zone two it should be located to insure nothing is wrong.

Buffer Reporting

Figure 6.11 shows a buffer report for a constraint where the buffer is equal to 16 hours. Each zone is 5 hours and 20 minutes. Zone one is from 151/0:00 to 151/5:20. Zone two is from 151/5:21 until 152/2:41. Zone three is from 152/2:42 until 153/0:02. Highlighted orders are ones which have arrived at the buffer origin.

Notice that KAB/20 for S/O 126 has not arrived at the constraint and it's due to start prior to 151/5:20, the designated ending for zone one. A quick look at the preceding part/operation's Inventory should help to locate the material and to expedite. If the material has not reached the constraint before the previous order has been completed the next order on the list should be processed instead to prevent loosing Throughput.

Managing the Buffer

What is needed now is a method for determining whether current protection is adequate and where to focus activities to improve. Figure 6.12 is a graphical representation of a buffer cross section frozen in time with each zone representing 2 hours.

Z N	Sales Order	Ord. Due	Part/ Oper.	Proc. Qty.	INV	Setup Time	Proc. Time	Start Time	End Time
1	8/0124	153	ABC/20	4	4	15	40	151/0:00	151/0:55
1	8/0124	153	DEF/20	4	4	15	40	151/0:56	151/1:51
1	8/0125	153	KAB/20	4	4	15	80	151/0:52	151/3:26
1	S/0126	153	KAB/20	4	0	15	80	151/3:27	151/5:02
1	8/0127	153	ABC/20	4	4	15	40	151/5:03	151/5:58
2	8/0127	153	DEF/20	4	4	15	40	151/5:59	151/6:54
2	S/0128	154	KAB/20	5	1	15	100	151/6:55	152/0:50
2	8/0129	154	ABC/20	5	5	15	50	152/0:51	152/1:56
2	S/0129	154	DEF/20	5	0	15	50	152/1:57	152/3:02
3	S/0130	154	KAB/20	4	0	15	80	152/3:03	152/4:38
3	S/0131	154	ABC/20	5	0	15	50	152/4:39	152/5:44
3	S/0131	154	DEF/20	5	0	15	50	152/5:45	152/6:50
3	S/0132	155	KAB/20	4	0	15	80	152/6:51	153/0:26

Figure 6.11 The buffer report.

```
      III              II              I
60 ┌─────┬─────┬─────┬─────┬─────┐
   │ 115 │ 114 │ 109 │ 108 │ 103 │
45 │     │     ├─────┤     ├─────┤  102
   │     │     │ 110 │     │ 104 │
30 ├─────┤ 113 ├─────┤ 107 ├─────┤  101
   │ 116 │     │     │     │     │
15 │ 117 │ 112 │ 111 │ 106 │ 105 │  100
   └─────┴─────┴─────┴─────┴─────┘
   12:00       10:00       8:00       6:00  (Buffer Origin)
```

Figure 6.12 The graphical representation of the buffer.

Each block represents an order and the timing of the order in crossing the buffer origin. The numbers at the left represent minutes. The numbers at the bottom represent hours. The first part of order 100 was scheduled to cross the constraint at 6:00 and be completed at 6:17. Order 109 was to start at 9:00 and run until 9:15. The bold print indicates that an order has arrived at the buffer origin while normal print indicates that an order has not arrived.

Different zone profiles will indicate different problems. Figure 6.13 indicates that all but two orders within the entire buffer have arrived leading to the conclusion that the six hour buffer may be too long.

Figure 6.14 indicates that very few have arrived leading to the conclusion that the buffer needs to be over 6 hours.

```
      III              II              I
60 ┌─────┬─────┬─────┬─────┬─────┐
   │ 115 │ 114 │ 109 │ 108 │ 103 │
45 │     │     ├─────┤     ├─────┤  102
   │     │     │ 110 │     │ 104 │
30 ├─────┤ 113 ├─────┤ 107 ├─────┤  101
   │ 116 │     │     │     │     │
15 │ 117 │ 112 │ 111 │ 106 │ 105 │  100
   └─────┴─────┴─────┴─────┴─────┘
   12:00       10:00       8:00       6:00  (Buffer Origin)
```

Figure 6.13 Buffer too long.

```
      III              II              I
60 ┌─────┬─────┬─────┬─────┬─────┐
   │ 115 │ 114 │ 109 │ 108 │ 103 │
45 │     │     ├─────┤     ├─────┤  102
   │     │     │ 110 │     │ 104 │
30 ├─────┤ 113 ├─────┤ 107 ├─────┤  101
   │ 116 │     │     │     │     │
15 │ 117 │ 112 │ 111 │ 106 │ 105 │  100
   └─────┴─────┴─────┴─────┴─────┘
   12:00       10:00       8:00       6:00  (Buffer Origin)
```

Figure 6.14 Buffer too short.

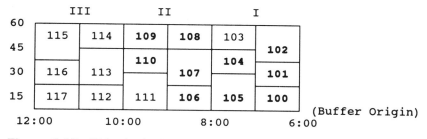

Figure 6.15 Holes in the buffer.

Figure 6.15 has a hole in the buffer where order 103 is missing, leading to the conclusion that some problem caused it to be late and that it needs to be expedited.

If material is arriving which is not due within any of the zones it means that material release may be uncontrolled. See figure 6.16.

Individual buffer profiles can be reduced to percentage figures to indicate the health of the buffer profile. In figure 6.17, after comparing the time parts were supposed to arrive with the actual time of arrival it is found that 90% of the orders have arrived by the beginning of zone one and that 75% of the orders have arrived before the beginning of zone two. This means that 10% of the orders are being expedited.

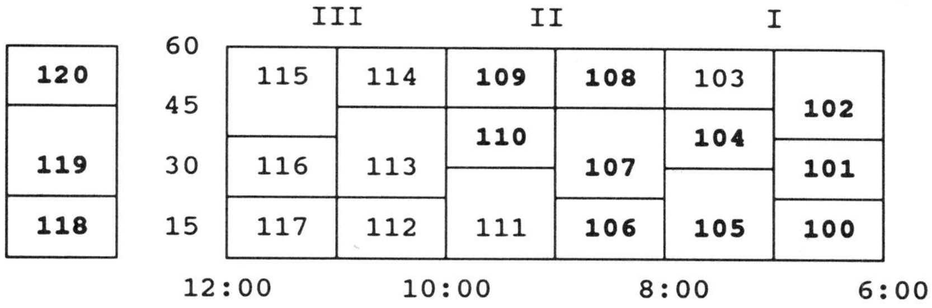

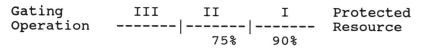

Figure 6.16 Material released too early.

```
Gating        III        II         I       Protected
Operation   -------|-------|-------   Resource
                        75%        90%
```

Figure 6.17 Buffer analysis by zone.

Individual companies may find that this situation is acceptable. However, finding that zone one had a 60% rating may not be tolerable and is a signal that either the amount of protection allowed should increase resulting in material being released earlier and an increase in Inventory or that whatever was causing the delays be eliminated or its impact reduced.

Measuring the Impact

Anytime an order has failed to arrive at the buffer origin by the beginning of zone one and has been expedited, a note made as to the cause of the delay and its location should be made. These causes should be collated by location and a Pareto analysis done of those instances that impact Throughput the most. To understand the total impact on Throughput, these occurrences should be dollarized. To emphasize the amount of lateness, time should be used. The resulting formula is the dollar amount of the sales order to be impacted minus the raw material value times the number of days late or "Throughput Dollar Days".

`Throughput x days late`

Throughput Dollar Days are collected by location, by occurrence. Those resources and occurrences collecting the most Throughput Dollar Days are the primary focus for improvements which should result in reducing Inventory while increasing the amount of protection available.

It may not always be possible to fix the exact problem which caused the delay. However, any method used to increase the amount of protective capacity available may offset for the problem. For example, a specific rework problem is causing a delay in material getting to the constraining resource prior to zone one. The rework is being caused by the lack of a fixture on a certain machine which may take some time before it can be replaced. However, unloading material to another machine which has excess capacity may release enough protective capacity to deal with this problem.

The Buffer Management Worksheet

Buffer Management Worksheets are organized to facilitate quantitative analysis and to insure uniformity in data collection. Whenever a part fails to reach the buffer origin prior to the beginning of the expedite zone, it is expedited and the cause and location of the delay are recorded along with the amount of lateness incurred. This information is used in the Pareto analysis phase to determine what actions must be taken to reduce the amount of protection necessary and is an adaptation of the standard checksheet used to collect data and to quantify the type of defect.

Buffer Management Worksheet

Buffer Origin: ___Resource C_____   Date: ___10/25/91__

Buffer Length: _16hrs   Zone Distribution: I 75% II 90%

Name: _John Smith_____

Loc	Station		Cause	Zone I Arr.	Act. Arr.
R-1	123/30	_____	Solder _____	154/2:15	154/5:15_
R-1	123/20	_____	Keyway _____	154/3:30	154/3:45_
R-2	121/30	_____	Out Mat. _____	154/5:10	154/7:10_
R-3	126/40	_____	Rework _____	155/1:30	155/2:30_
R-1	131/20	_____	Mach Dwn _____	155/2:30	155/3:30_

The buffer origin designates the location of the buffer at a specific resource or at shipping. The buffer length gives the buffer manager an indication of the buffer length used at this particular operation so that an idea of the amount of protection given can be established. The zone distribution gives the buffer manager an idea of the health of the system prior to the buffer origin.

Buffer Management Reports

While the buffer management worksheet is used to collect data and can give a certain amount of insight as to the health of the system, some idea of the relative impact of an occurrence must be gaged by its impact on the bottom line. The Buffer Management Report takes the input from the Buffer Management Worksheet and determines the relative impact by injecting the Throughput Dollar and Inventory Dollar Day equation.

Pareto Analysis

The Pareto Analysis is a specific type of histogram which gives an instantaneous picture of the priorities for improvement projects based on past history. The source of data is the buffer management worksheet and is used to separate the "vital few" resources and causes, which create the majority of Throughput/Inventory Dollar Days (T/I$D), from the "trivial many". Pareto analysis can be accomplished two ways; the first is to discern which resources are collecting the most Throughput Dollar Days and then to prioritize problems within each resource which caused the T/I$D to accumulate. Figure 6.18 illustrates.

Buffer Management Report

Buffer Origin: ___R-5_____   Date: ___10/25/91__

Buffer Length: _16hrs   Zone Distribution: I 75% II 90%

Name: _John Smith_____

Loc	Station	Cause	Length	(T) Value	T$D
R-1	123/30	Solder	0.5 Days x	$1,000	= 500
R-1	131/20	Keyway	1.0 Day x	$2,000	= 2,000
R-2	121/30	Out Mat.	2.0 Days x	$1,500	= 3,000
R-3	126/40	Rework	1.0 Days x	$2,500	= 2,500
R-5	123/30	Rework	0.5 Days x	$1,000	= 500
R-1	131/20	Marking	1.0 Day x	$2,000	= 2,000
R-2	121/30	Rework	2.0 Days x	$1,000	= 2,000
R-5	126/40	Rework	1.0 Days x	$2,500	= 2,500
R-1	123/30	Rework	0.5 Days x	$1,000	= 500
R-1	131/20	Marking	1.0 Day x	$2,000	= 2,000

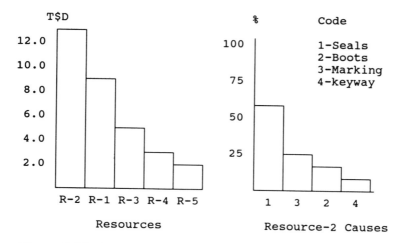

Figure 6.18 Pareto Analysis by Throughput dollar days.

Obviously, the majority of T$D are being accumulated by resource R-2. A further Pareto analysis of the causes reveals that 55% of the delays were related to seals.

The Shop Floor Layout

Once the method of scheduling a factory for maximizing productivity has been found, some insight can be gained toward the shape of the factory floor. While every manufacturing facility will be different, some similarities will definitely apply. The biggest change will be in the area of material location and in the provisions made to accommodate volume. In those areas directly in front of the constraint(s), shipping and assembly operations where one leg is fed by the constraint there will be a moderate amount of Inventory buildup. Inventory must be stored in such a way as to allow easy access for the implementation of buffer management. For those areas not located at the constraint, requirements for Inventory storage will be relatively negligible. Material will be passing these locations very quickly and in small quantities. Figure 6.19 illustrates.

Resource 6 has been identified as the constraint, so the buffer area has been established at this location. Buffers have also been created in front of shipping and in front of resource 9. This particular layout does not preclude the use of other techniques for increasing efficiency by lowering the amount of distance traveled such as U-lines or Group Technology (GT) cells. Resource 6 may be a U-line while resource 5 may be a GT cell. However, it must be remembered that converting to a process of higher efficiency on resources with excess capacity may actually result in a decline of profitability.

Rules for Non-Constraint Resource Utilization

Under the DBR process the amount of Inventory in non-constraint resources will be very low. The method of determining priority is first in first out (FIFO). Since the schedule for the constraint and the amount of protection required determines

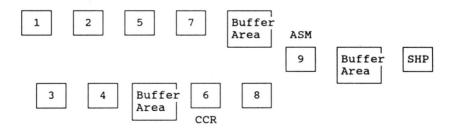

Figure 6.19   The shop floor layout. CCR = capacity-constrained resource.

the release date, the sequencing of orders has already been determined and should be by arrival date/time to the non-constraints. Unless there is a problem causing an order to penetrate zone one in buffer management, no effort is made to change this rule. Resources are activated when material is available for work, and deactivated when no material is available. Employees not having work in there area should spend time on employee involvement programs. However, they must be available immediately if work does arrive in their area. The work should be completed as fast as possible and sent to the next operation.

DBR in the Office Environment

Resources tend to interact the same regardless of the environment. An engineer may produce a different product than a lathe, but, he can be considered a constraint, near-constraint or a non-constraining resource. While scheduling a factory and scheduling a group of engineers may seem worlds apart, from that perspective they are, in fact, one and the same. And so, the same problems will occur in much the same way as in the factory and should be dealt with in the same manner. If the objective is to maximize productivity from engineering then that resource (engineer) which is limiting output must be exploited and all other resources must be subordinated to the way in which it is decided to exploit the engineers time. If an engineer who is in a critical position whithin the design process is slow or lacks the knowledge needed to complete designs quickly, this will present a problem in increasing the volume of the overall design process. At the same time, an engineer who is fast and knowledgeable but has excess capacity may be used to increase capacity at the constraint.

Problems in lead time reduction would involve the same strategy as buffer management where those things which threaten the schedule for the constraint are identified by zone. While few companies have created route files and bills of material for the design process, most engineering projects include some indication of the amount of time required for completing each design or group of designs and a basic sequencing. There should be enough information to create a product flow diagram and a schedule. As in the factory, a physical constraint can be identified using effect-cause-effect and by experiment.

In an area such as accounts payable little information is available for indicating the amount of time it should take to enter an invoice. However, most clerks can tell you exactly how long it takes. The sequencing of operations is usually very simple and well established.

Remember, implementing DBR in accounts payable or engineering just to improve the process may do nothing to increase profitability. There is, however, a growing issue over the shelf life of products and the speed at which designs are created and become obsolete. This is a strategic issue and must be addressed. The DBR process will help immensely in being able to overcome problems in reducing design times by isolating those problems which will contribute immediately to the increase in design volume and to the reduction of design lead time. This is a key issue and must be addressed whether or not designs are immediately blocking the increase of Throughput entering the company.

The DBR Advantage

Dr. Ohno, one of the creators of the Just-in-time process, has been quoted as not knowing why his process worked, only that it does. The developers of the DBR system understood the impact of the dependent variable environment and constraint management on the scheduling/improvement process and incorporated it to create a system which has been proven far superior to other programs not just for scheduling the factory but for improving profits. While understanding the impact of the dependent variable environment on being able to produce a solution to the scheduling process and having a smooth product flow is important the objective of the company is still to make money. The DBR process was designed to support this objective and therefor represents a tremendous advantage.

- The advantages include:
- Less Inventory
- The improvement process is more efficient and predictable
- Flexibility
- Less vulnerable to *Murphy*
- Shorter Implementation period
- Better manageability
- Higher Throughput
- Enhances the decision making process
- Supports and implements the five step process

7

The Attributes of TQM II

In this chapter the process of developing a larger perspective to the overall scope of TQM II and to identify its attributes is begun.

OBJECTIVES

- To introduce the principles and key components of the TQM II system.
- To establish the TQM II strategy and requirements.
- To define quality as a necessary condition and to understand why companies fail to meet their customers quality demands.

THE TQM II OBJECTIVE

The objective of TQM II is to establish an effective management system designed to implement the process of continuous profit improvement while meeting the necessary condition of good quality.

THE TQM II PRINCIPLES

The principles of TQMII serve as guidelines to help in understanding how to focus efforts in maximizing profitability through the implementation of the TQM II program. A violation of these principles will result in less than desirable effects.

Principle 1.   Quality is a necessary condition.

The perception of quality for money spent is a condition which must be met before most people will buy a particular product. While an increase in quality will not always guarantee an increase in profitability, the condition of quality has a regulatory effect which, if not continually met, will definitely result in a decline.

Principle 2.   Every solution will serve to invalidate itself over time.

Any solution which may have been valid at the time it was implemented, will serve to invalidate itself once it has solved the particular problem it was designed to fix. If the problem is a flat tire and the solution is to mount a spare, once the spare tire has been mounted, the problem as well as the solution are no longer in effect. While this seems like a trivial matter, when applied to the chain of events which occur in a company it means that once a problem has been solved a program of continually looking for the next one to surface is mandatory. In the spare tire analogy, continually driving from store to store buying a new and better tire to replace the one which went flat would ultimately result in bankruptcy. Continually massaging the cost accounting issue even though it has ceased to solve any problems may result in bankruptcy as well.

Principle 3.   The Throughput of the system is determined by its constraints.

As seen in the description of the process of "continuous profit improvement", companies represent a chain of events. In any chain there is a weak link. It is the weak links which determine how much money can be generated.

Principle 4.   The value of an activity is determined by the limitations of the system.

It is the limitations of the system that ultimately determine how much money a company can make. Any activity must be weighed based on it's impact on those limitations. Value is not determined by the frequency or the cost of the occurrence. An improvement in a resource which has excess capacity will not by itself result in an increase in the profitability of the company but, may actually result in a decrease in profitability.

Principle 5.   The utilization of any resource may be determined by any other resource in a chain of events.

It is the interactions between resources and ultimately customer or forecasted demand which determines the extent of utilization. However, since each resource is used collectively to produce an effect in satisfying the customer if one resource does not perform its specific function it will ultimately block the creation of Throughput.

Principle 6.   The level of Inventory and Operating Expense is determined by the attributes of the non-constraints.

Inventory and Operating Expense exist to create or protect Throughput. It is the characteristics of the non-constraints which determine how much protection is actually required. A decrease in protection due to a lack of capacity at a non-constraint resource results in an increase in inventory as jobs must be released earlier. Operating expense goes up as overtime is needed to catch up. Material arriving late to the constraint did so because of a problem at non-constraint, whether it be the vendor for late material or a production resource due to a quality problem.

Principle 7.   Resources are to be utilized in the creation or protection of Throughput, not merely activated.

Activating resources to produce inventory which is not needed to create Throughput will ultimately result in an increase in inventory. An increase in inventory will cause profits to decline. However, the major problem is the impact on Throughput. As Inventories go up lead times are extended and Throughput declines.

THE KEY COMPONENTS OF TQM II

TQM II is a very broad system of management which includes:

1. An orientation toward "continuous profit improvement".
2. A valid decision support mechanism.
3. A customer oriented quality focus.
4. Local measurements which are in line with global measurements.
5. A people oriented management system.
6. A team approach to problem solving.
7. A company wide focus on the five steps of improvement.
8. The religious use of Effect-Cause-Effect, Assumption Modeling, Positive Trees, Prerequisite Trees and Action Plans in problem resolution at all levels.
9. A program of supplier involvement and cooperation.
10. An internal orientation toward customer-supplier relationships.
11. A valid method of focusing improvement programs.
12. The use of statistical as well as fail-safing methods for controlling processes
13. Long term business focus and commitment.
14. A prevention oriented quality program.
15. An unencumbered network of information exchange.
16. A valid scheduling mechanism.
17. A controlled program of variation reduction.
18. A fully integrated system of profit improvement and quality management.
19. An empowering approach to employee involvement.
20. Tailor-made management and control strategies.
21. Employee based process ownership and commitment.
22. A dynamic system for learning, managing and adapting to change.
23. Comprehensive and well focused education and training.

THE TQM II REQUIREMENTS

- Top management leadership and commitment
- Employee involvement and human resource excellence.
- A Throughput orientation toward "continuous profit improvement".
- An orientation toward customer satisfaction.

The Key TQM II Strategy: Team problem solving utilizing self-direct worker and management teams and valid/well focused improvement processes and control mechanisms.

DEFINING THE KEY COMPONENTS

1. An orientation toward continuous profit improvement.

The objective of most companies is to make money. A healthy company is able to grow continuously. The TQM II system focuses on growing a company and focusing efforts on continually increasing profits.

2. A valid decision support mechanism.

Making valid decisions is the cornerstone to being able to manage any company. As long as decisions are continuously made which are in line with the global goals and objectives of the company the chances of success are far greater. Making valid decisions requires having access to valid data upon which to base the decision. The traditional decision support systems (via cost accounting) fall very much short of being able to accomplish this task. What is necessary is a complete re-thinking of what is called an information system and what is merely a data system. As an example, what information is necessary to make the decision of what product mix would maximize the profitability of the company? Traditionally, the equation has been based on the cost of goods sold, using various overhead allocation models. Emphasis was placed on understanding what the "true cost" of a product actually is and then subtracting that from the sales price. The product which had the largest margin was considered the most profitable regardless of how much money could actually be made given the limitations provided by the environment. In the section on Correcting the Decision Process in Chapter five it was found that the information which was actually required was very much different than what is traditionally used. Based on the Throughput generated per unit of the constraint what is actually needed from the decision support system to make the decision for product mix is:

- The identification of the constraint.
- The cost of raw material.
- What the product is being sold for.
- How much time is used by the constraint in making the part.

While most standard systems can provide details on the cost of raw material, the sales price and the amount of constraint time used, few are capable of actually finding the systems constraints.

3. A customer oriented quality focus.

The first step in meeting the necessary condition of good quality is to determine and set the quality policy. It is the customer who buys the products and therefore determines what level of quality is required. The quality policy determines to what level the necessary condition is to be met. The quality function deployment program focuses the customers desires onto the processes and sets the standards to which resources are expected to perform. Once the quality policy has been set it is the visible and obvious management commitment from the top which generates waves of commitment and quality attitude throughout the company. This, when supported by a clear and concise program of assigning quality objectives and the active elimination of the root causes for failing to meet customer expectation will result in the necessary condition being fulfilled.

(Note: When a quality policy of meeting the necessary condition is not matched with a process of continuous profit improvement the enthusiasm for maintaining the necessary condition will die.)

Management as well as employees will abandon those activities which do not lead to satisfying the profit requirement.

4. Local measurements which are in line with global measurements.

The necessity of local measurements upon which to build a valid decision system that will impact the global measurements correctly must be met for any system to produce the desired results. The establishment of Throughput, Inventory and Operating Expense provides an intuitive as well as emperical basis for making local decisions and for focusing the improvement process.

5. A people oriented management system.

The TQM II process requires a people oriented management system which is designed to instill self-ownership. Authoritarian management styles do not effectively support a process of continuous profit or process improvement. The short term benefits of any fear or shame tactics will soon give way to long term negative effects. People can only be threatened with losing their jobs for a short period of time before they begin responding in ways which are non-productive. Management must be committed to solving problems not assessing blame. Managers must learn to lead people either through group or individual activity by having them invent their own solutions so that the effects of the fear and "not invented here" emotions will be minimized. The TQM II management style is an open management process with clear and consistent objectives, well communicated and effectively explained to all. Emphasis is placed on a group derived improvement process through open forums and the elimination of adversarial conditions and "elitist" management attitudes.

An effective TQM II management program will use effective combinations of motivational (humanistic) and scientific (quantitative) elements to effect control by "choice" rather than control by edict (force).

Trust is a key issue. Employees and managers alike should be allowed to do their jobs without people looking over their shoulders. A committed management will be actively involved in helping employees do their jobs, but from a supporting role. The positive effects of having the president of a company visible on the shop floor just to listen to people problems is well documented and since employees tend to model the attitudes and behaviors of management it is a great opportunity for an infusion of good will and TQM II world thinking into the lower levels of the corporation.

6. A team approach to problem solving.

It has been often said that the whole is greater than the sum of its parts and in managing complex organizations the most effective way to tap a companies human resources is through the use of self directed worker and management teams where the generation of concepts and new ideas can be developed, fostered and implemented, and where manager and worker involvement/cooperation can be perpetuated. TQM II uses a team approach to bridge the interface between functional disciplines and eliminate the natural antagonism caused by different functional goals and work procedures. TQM II supports problem solving as well as long and short range planning through the rigorous use of problem solving tools in group forums such as:

- The TQM II Executive Council.
- The Quality Management Council.
- Cross Functional Management Teams.
- Project Teams.
- Employee Involvement Teams.

7. A company wide focus on the five steps of improvement as presented in chapter one.

It is obvious that to produce a process of "continuous profit improvement" a system of identifying the constraint and determining how to exploit it, subordinating the remaining resources to those activities designed to protect the constraint and then elevating and repeating the process must be understood and carried out by everyone in the company. Since every company is a chain of events, any function within the organization can block the process which improves the amount of Throughput being generated. Therefore everyone within the company must be exposed to the process and support it religiously.

8. The religious use of Effect-Cause-Effect, Assumption Modeling, Positive Trees, Prerequisite Trees and Action Plans in problem resolution at all levels.

Being able to create a process of "continuous profit improvement" means being able to find the constraint and then create and implement simple solutions which can be easily understood. Since 90% of a systems constraints will be policy oriented and not redily identifiable, and since most constraints will be caused by erroneous or outdated thinking, it is essential that a system be implemented which organizes and focuses the thought process and then directs actions toward solving the core problem.

- Effect-Cause-Effect—Used to identify core problems.
- Assumption Modeling—Used to break the assumptions causing the erroneous thinking which created the core problem.
- Positive Trees—Used to predict the outcome of a specific change.
- Prerequisite trees—Used to understand what the prerequisites are to accomplishing a specific change.
- Action Plans—Used to determine what actions must occur to accomplish the prerequisites to the change.

9. A program of supplier involvement and cooperation.

Every supplier's operation should be considered as an extension of the manufacturing facility and treated as such. Suppliers are valuable partners in business who can help tremendously in accomplishing the ultimate goal of implementing a process of "continuous profit improvement". Relationships should be based on mutual interest and trust not antagonism and distrust.

10. An internal orientation toward customer-supplier.

Every worker should think of themselves as both supplier as well as customer in the chain of events leading to the creation of Throughput and act accordingly. As these relationships manifest themselves worker attitudes and habits begin to change. The self checking and next process inspection procedures act to reenforce the quality of work from each resource by giving immediate feedback to the process responsible for creating the defect. Each resource uses a short checklist to validate whether the work performed at the resource meets a certain level of quality before it is sent on and has a separate checklist for validating that the work received from the previous resource meets certain quality levels. Each list is not extensive and adds very little to the overall work load. Since most resources will be non-constraints there will be no additional Operating Expense. The benefit is that this procedure enhances the smooth flow of material through the plant and creates additional visibility when trying to determine the cause of holes appearing in zone one of the buffer management system. It also insures that a large number of people have viewed the quality of work performed before constraint time is wasted.

11. A valid method of focusing improvement programs.

Variation reduction, setup reduction, total productive maintenance, engineering improvements, and marketing programs all need ways of focusing to insure that their results will have a positive and immediate impact on profitability. TQM II provides a valid method of focus with profitability as the ultimate goal.

12. The use of statistical as well as fail-safing methods for controlling processes.

Once an assignment of resource capability requirements have been made by either the deployment of customer requirements via the quality function deployment system or the impact of demand on the relationship between resources, the degree of process control necessary can be determined. The regular use of statistical methods, such as Statistical Process Control (SPC) and Design of Experiments (see Chapters 8 and 10) (DOE), as well as fail-safing methods (Poka Yoke) to control processes will help to insure that:

- Resources are kept under control so that necessary conditions will be met.
- A maximum exploitation of the constraint or the effective subordination of non-constraint resources will occur.

If a process is under control it is producing the best that it can produce without modification. Statistical methods help to determine when a process is out of control now or due to go out of control in the future and give an indication of what may be wrong so that corrective action can be taken.

13. Long term business focus and commitment.

American business has long been forced, for various reasons, to adopt a policy of focusing on the quarterly report to judge what actions are necessary to maintain a profit. And, for most businesses this is a fact of life which will not go away. However, when the focus is one of short term cost reduction measures and not one which concentrates on Throughput management the results are no less than catastrophic. How can a company fulfill the necessary condition of good quality and implement the five steps of improvement if it is narrowly focused on cost reduction. Because of a lack of a continuous profit improvement program, companies have had no choice but to be short sighted. But, to sacrifice the future of the company to make the numbers look good today simply defies all logic. What should happen to every company that is successful at fulfilling the customers requirements while implementing the five stepped process is that the quarterly focus problem goes away. It has become increasingly evident that it is possible to focus on short term profits as well as long term issues at the same time. But it must be done correctly.

14. A prevention oriented quality program.

Any attempt to fulfill the necessary condition of good quality must be defect prevention oriented. It has been proven over and over again that quality cannot be inspected into a product. To be effective the focus must be on preventing mistakes from occurring in the first place. Products arriving to the constraint which have defects and use constraint time only to be scrapped will cause Throughput to decline immediately and that amount of Throughput is not recoverable. Relying only on an inspection process in front of the constraint to catch defective parts would mean that an unacceptable number of defective parts would reach the constraint. A prevention oriented quality program would use process control methods such as SPC and Fail-safing to control the process. It would also use robust designs which are well within process capabilities.

15. An unencumbered network of information exchange.

Blocking the flow of information will ultimately effect a companies ability to respond correctly by distorting reality. Making correct decisions and supporting a process of continuous profit improvement requires that the decision process be based on reality. Distorting reality means distorting the decision process which will ultimately hurt the profitability of the company.

16. A valid scheduling mechanism.

To be able to identify the limitations of the system now as well as in the future and therefore to support the decision process requires that the demand of each resource be known for the period of time for which the decision is to be made. To do this a valid scheduling mechanism must be available which will place the load giving consideration for the limitations of the system and the relationship between resources.

17. A controlled program of variation reduction.

Getting as close to the target value is the objective of any SPC or TQM program. However, variation reduction for the sake of reducing variability by itself is not desirable. It should be part of an overall program of insuring the current as well as future profitability of the company by fulfilling the necessary condition now as well as in the future and as part of the five step process.

18. A fully integrated system of profit improvement and quality management.

It is obvious that what every company needs is a well focused system for managing a program of "continuous profit improvement" and for fulfilling the "necessary condition" of good quality. TQM II provides a fully integrated system for accomplishing these objectives by insuring that:

- Every employee within the company knows what is expected and every activity is correctly focused.
- Valid measurement systems provide a solid basis for decisions.
- Everyone is able to participate in the process and understands what the indicators of success or failure are.

19. An empowering approach to employee involvement.

It is the employees who determine the success or failure of any company and who hold the key to understanding what actions are occurring in reality. But often it is the chain of communication and the lack of ability to take actions which hamper any management strategy. Empowerment means giving employees the power to make decisions and take corrective actions where necessary to get the job done.

20. Tailor-made management and control strategies.

Every company is different with respect to the problems encountered and the solutions required. TQM II recognizes that to be effective an innovative approach is necessary rather than a correlative approach of implementation. Implementing the same solutions as another company may miss the target altogether and result in the loss of money and not improvement.

21. Employee based process ownership and commitment.

Each process is identified and assigned an owner who is ultimately responsible for insuring that his process is properly exploited, if it is the constraint, subordinated, if it is a non-constraint, or that the quality characteristics assigned to it by the QFD program are met. Meaurement systems are also assigned emphasizing the committment to global issues.

22. A dynamic system for learning, managing and adapting to change.

Change, being inevitable and often illusive, requires a system of management which constantly shifts to meet its needs. The TQM II system recognizes that any solution will become invalid over time and therefore must be capable of reacting to whatever change may occur. It must also recognize that while change is inevitable peoples resistance to change is also inevitable and be prepared to prevent resistance.

23. Comprehensive and well focused education and training.

Education is a tool used not just to dispense information but to motivate and to attempt to have people capable of inventing their own solutions. When the learning process stops companies begin to stagnate and ultimately fail to continue the processes that will help them the most. TQM II includes a life long commitment to training and education.

QUALITY AS A NECESSARY CONDITION

Poor quality is like inadequate cash flow. Whenever a company cannot find money in adequate amounts necessary to pay its debts, the decision process becomes skewed to the extent that it becomes a primary consideration in almost every decision. The residual effects of solving the cash flow problem but still dealing with vendors who are hesitant to ship because of poor payment records can be just as disastrous. Companies who have found additional cash to feed the operation are still faced with poor credit. Vendors who have spent a large amount of time trying to get paid are hesitant to ship for fear of losing more money. If vendors won't ship obviously customer orders cannot be filled causing more cash flow problems. It is a vicious circle no company wants to face.

Like poor cash flow, the effects of a customers perception of poor quality will have an immediate impact on sales but it will also produce long lasting residual effects. It may be more expensive and take more time to change a customers perception than to actually increase product quality. Poor quality is a competitive edge issue which cannot be ignored. While good quality will not always increase the amount of money coming into a company, poor quality will definitely have a negative impact which can last for a long period of time. Product quality is a necessary condition and therefore should not be allowed to become the constraint to making more money.

MEETING THE NECESSARY CONDITION

The objective in meeting the necessary condition of good quality is to build and deliver products which meet customer expectations or requirements. To do this means being able to:

- Know what the customer requirements are and to convert them into product and process specifications.
- Have processes capable of meeting customer requirements.
- Eliminate the blockers to meeting the necessary condition.

The traditional causes for failure to fulfill the quality requirements of customers are quite large including:

- Preoccupation with short term profits and corporate mergers.
- Using sales gimmicks as a substitute for solid quality thereby setting customer perceptions which will not be met.
- Not focusing on customer satisfaction.
- Preoccupation with limiting customer complaints rather than focusing on customer satisfaction.
- Lack of effective planning for long term stability.
- Failure to utilize the inherent abilities of workers to contribute to process improvement.
- A culture permeated by attitudes of mistrust.
- Massive bureaucracies with intricate checks and balances for controlling every action.
- A focus on failure, with elaborate procedures for assessing punishment.

- Management inconsistency toward quality.
- Elitism as a tool for management control.
- The tendency to inspect defects out rather than building quality in.
- Rigid systems which fight change.
- Placing increased pressure on productivity without first correcting the problem.
- Cutting expenses arbitrarily.
- A dependence upon authoritarian management and single-track, single minded, structures for control.
- Antagonistic relationships with suppliers—price competition instead of cooperation—large supplier bases.
- Internal function oriented, rather than customer oriented, goals.

While the symptoms and surface causes for failure to meet customer expectations can be very broad, the root causes are few. They include:

- Conflicting goals and measurements.
- Poor decision systems and support mechanisms.
- Lack of understanding of how to meet the necessary conditions.
- A lack of understanding of how resources interface and the resulting impact on the system.
- The cost mentality.
- Failure to understand how to motivate people.

Of all the causes probably the biggest problems to meeting the necessary conditions set by the customer and for meeting the profit objectives of companies stem from conflicting goals and measurements as well as poor or invalid decision systems and support mechanisms. Conflicting goals and measurements will result in organizations optimizing certain departments at the expense of others. As an example, the purchasing manager may be measured based on performance to standard cost. The management objective being to constantly reduce the cost of raw material coming into the plant. The net result may be a large number of vendors, a high degree of variability in raw material and lower quality parts. The end result of which is massive interruptions, an inability to successfully exploit the constraint or to properly subordinate the efforts of other resources and a reduction in overall profitability. The purchasing manager gets a raise right before the plant closes.

The preoccupation with short term profit objectives is usually a direct result of a failure to meet acceptable profit levels. Poor decision systems and support mechanisms will create a situation where poor profit is a constant problem. The resulting turmoil will create constant shortages of qualified people to produce quality products as well as a morale problem with people constantly looking over their shoulder for fear that they may be laid off next. Poor support mechanisms such as the method used for scheduling the factory will result in less than desirable results as well. At the first of the month the pressure for delivery may be low. However, if a poor scheduling system results in a large backlog of late orders, meeting the necessary conditions of the customer may be in conflict with the obligations of the company in meeting investor and creditor requirements. High quality parts are delivered at the first of the month and low quality parts are delivered at the end of the month.

A continuous focus on ways of reducing cost to meet profitability goals (the cost mentality) can play havoc on a company's ability to meet quality requirements even when a company is not having a perceived profit problem. Employees are easily equated to cost outlets rather than opportunities for creating Throughput. This kind of attitude is quickly picked up by employees and transmitted to their work. Whenever cost is the number one issue cutting corners becomes easier to justify. Required maintenance is overlooked or the need for a new tool is ignored.

Not understanding how resources interface and what the impact of a decision is from a global perspective can result in improvements being made in the wrong areas or a total misunderstanding of how to schedule a production facility.

Without knowing what a customer needs, it is very difficult to fulfill the necessary condition. Failure to implement a program which details customer requirements, translates them into designs and product specifications and then into process specifications will insure that the companies product planning efforts will remain hit or miss. If quality is considered to be a necessary condition then this must occur.

The cost mentality is any learned response which serves to block the ability to look at reality in a common sense fashion. It is the basis for most policy constraints and is probably the number one cause for not being able to implement a process of continuous profit improvement. It is the ultimate cause of conflicting goals and objectives as well as invalid decision systems.

CONTINUOUS PRODUCT IMPROVEMENT PROGRAMS

The degree of improvement of a product is a strategic issue and whether or not a process of "continuous" improvement is carried out depends on its strategic implications. To ignore the improvement of a product in a highly competitive environment such as the computer industry, is courting certain death for the product line or company. What characteristics a product must have to be salable one to five years from now cannot be ignored in the present. Ignoring an improvement in a product until the last minute simply because it is not the constraint at this time or because the necessary condition is now being met and then expecting to be competitive in the future is like sitting on a train track while a train is coming and being happy because you haven't yet been hit. At the same time setting up a program of continuous improvement for a product whose life cycle is nearly spent or is expected to be stable for some time to come is probably a waste of time and money and will result in a decline of profitability. Where a company and its products must be in the future determines what improvement initiatives are implemented today. If it is expected that defect rates will need to be lower in the future then a program of constantly reducing variability may be necessary. If it is expected that products will need to be faster or smaller then a process of constantly improving the product will be necessary so that necessary conditions can be met in the future. The quality strategy should include a decision to support or not support continuous product improvement and if so the degree of continuous improvement necessary.

PROCESS VARIABILITY

Process variation in manufacturing is inevitable. It is virtually impossible to create two objects which are exactly the same. It is the frequency and degree of variation which may have tremendous impact on the quality of products produced and the Throughput generated. Under traditional TQM, the objective of the statistical sciences is to track and support the reduction of the amount of variation which occurs in the system. Emphasis is placed on the magnitude and frequency of occurrence. The causes of abnormal variation for a manufacturing environment include man, material, machine, method and tooling. The causes of variation are further categorized into chance causes, which are considered normal, and assignable causes. Assignable causes create recognizable trends, are assumed to be correctable and is the subject of Statistical Process Control (SPC).

Under TQM II the degree of variability is not as important as its impact on Throughput, Inventory and Operating Expense. Variability is viewed as an issue under the five step improvement process. If it causes a constraint or restricts the ability to properly exploit and subordinate, its relative importance must be elevated above the normal programs dedicated to the control and reduction of variability within processes. Normal variability reduction programs should represent an ongoing process designed to prevent quality from becoming the constraint or to insure that the "necessary condition" is met as part of an overall strategic plan.

BREAKING THE NECESSARY CONDITION

In the event that quality has become the constraint, increasing quality may not be the immediate solution. Breaking the necessary condition may be more profitable in the short as well as long run. In other words, if the playing field is setup to play by a given set of rules, change the rules or find a game more to your liking using the resource capability you have. It is not necessary, nor often profitable to assume that the rules cannot be changed. The distinction must be made at this point that what is being advocated is not running from a quality issue but looking for places to find more money without limitations in thought.

If a machine shop is unable to keep up with the technology being requested from current customers, it may elect to find a segmented market where the level of technology is not as stringent and sell part of its resource time into that market while it is making the changes necessary to get back into the high technology market. Great care must be taken to insure that the level of quality is competitive and acceptable to the new customer base. Otherwise, management may find that they now have a bad name in two markets.

THE TEAM CONCEPT

Few would argue that as the size and complexity of businesses grow the ability to manage from a global perspective declines. While the effects may be devastating, the cause may simply be a decline in communication. Experience has shown that in the traditional company, the larger an organization, the more isolated its members. People become discouraged as communication drops off because they are unable to cope with the magnitude of the problems and because they do not feel a part of the process. Individual departments develop a myopic view of the world and are unable to function to maximize the whole of the organization. Managers as well as supervisors are forced to rely more and more on invalid localized measurements and decision mechanisms which can have a devastating impact on profitability.

While large companies may resemble lumbering dinosaurs, small companies represent cohesive entities. They become successful because management is able to readily view individual activities/decision processes and their impact on profitability from a global perspective. Communication is greatly enhanced by the smallness of the organizational structure where technology and information is easily shared.

It seems that what is needed for managing large companies is a method for increasing communication and individual worker input while focusing efforts to maximize profitability. Work teams revitalize the small company perspective by increasing communication and creating the opportunity to manage globally. They consist of 6 to 15 highly trained individuals with shared responsibility for a finished work segment. Each individual contributes to the whole by bringing his/her unique ability and by creating an entity which is greater than the some of its parts. Work teams take many forms including:

- Cross-functional management teams.
- Employee involvement teams.
- The TQM II Executive Council.
- Steering Committees.
- Self Directed Work Teams.

It is important to insure that each individual is able to contribute in a way which is constructive to the entire team. Each team member is trained not just on working with teams and team concepts such as brainstorming and effect-cause-effect but, time is given to insure that each member is technically qualified to contribute as well. Engineers are trained to be better engineers while quality, production and purchasing people are trained to understand more about their functions as well. Each must function with a valid decision making process and focusing mechanism.

How a specific team is used depends on what function they are asked to perform. A strategic decision to support a process of continuous product improvement will dictate that a different improvement process be used than a team whose function is to increase profitability. The benefits of using the team concept are increased communication, a ready access to highly qualified people, a better sense of self determination among the team members and a higher probability of problem resolution.

Developing the TQM II Infrastructure

In this chapter an infrastructure for the implementation and establishment of the improvement process is created.

OBJECTIVES

- To create the organizational/communications structure and assign responsibility.
- To establish insight into the documentation strategy for formalizing the process.
- To introduce the concept of feedback and control mechanisms in completing the communications structure and to understand how they are to be used under the TQM II strategy.

THE MANAGEMENT SYSTEM IMPERATIVES

To be effective any management system must have:

- An effective means of relaying information.
- A valid decision process.
- A valid set of measurements.
- An effective feedback mechanism.
- A method for identifying, prioritizing and solving problems.

Until now the text has been devoted to changing the paradigms associated with traditional Total Quality Management which deal with the decision process, measurement systems and methods for identifying, prioritizing and solving problems. What must now be addressed are methods of developing and maintaining communication such as the organizational structure, documentation and traditional feedback mechanisms which may or may not require enhancement to support a global perspective. Each of these issues must be addressed within the context of the five step improvement process.

THE TQM II ORGANIZATIONAL STRUCTURE

The first task in creating the TQM II management system will be to develop the organizational structure designed to support the system and to assign responsibilities. The organizational structure should promote effective communication between organizations and insure proper and timely feedback when problems occur. This will include:

- The TQM II Executive Council.
- The Quality Management Council.
- The Cross-functional Management Team.
- The Project Team.
- The Employee Involvment and Quality Circle Teams.

The TQM II Executive Council

The TQM II executive council consists of the top executives from the company including the president and representatives from the major functions of finance and accounting, manufacturing, engineering, quality, sales and marketing, distribution, and customer service. It is important for every function to be represented. Their responsibility is to formulate corporate policy and to oversee the program and it's implementation. From an executive level this group determines the direction the corporation will take in implementing the five step improvement process. This group actively participates in group sessions and routinely uses effect-cause-effect, assumption modeling, and positive as well as prerequisite trees in the development of the action plan. A group forum is important. While every participant should religiously prepare their own documentation, a group consensus can be developed by using these tools in open sessions while developing the corporate plan. The head of the TQM II executive council and primary facilitator should be the president of the corporation. This group determines the strategic directions the corporation will take and the way in which money will be spent. Elevation may mean buying a new machine worth millions of dollars or changing a major corporate policy. It is of prime importance that the chief executive for the corporation chair this event.

The Quality Management Council

The quality management council is established to insure that the quality of products and services being offered to customers are competitive by setting direction and establishing policy. It has the task of developing, assigning and monitoring major quality improvement projects and for providing support where necessary to maintain a process of on-going product or process improvement when necessary. The objective of the council is to prevent quality issues from becoming the constraint to making money. Among a number of different programs, the quality management council is responsible for the quality function deployment program and should be concerned about product safety, reliability, availability, maintainability and conformance to specification as well as customer perception. The quality management council develops, assigns and monitors quality improvement projects, works to identify and plan training requirements, sets measurement criteria, monitors the rewards management system and establishes and monitors the quality circles program.

Cross-Functional Management Teams

The cross-functional management team consists of managers from each function and has the responsibility to insure that the action plan set by the TQM II executive council and the quality management council is carried out. Activities are assigned to insure that the constraint is properly exploited and that all other activities are subordinated to it. The cross-functional management team offers quick access to all functions for faster action when problems occur and, when the constraint is elevated, it reduces the probability that inertia will cause problems by exposing a larger number of people and viewpoints to the same problems. The cross-functional management team will also use the effect-cause-effect, assumption model, and positive and prerequisite tree techniques in individual as well as group forum in the development of action plans and in solving problems.
(Note: In small companies, the TQM II Executive Council, Quality Management Council and Cross-Functional Management Teams may be the same people.)

The product design review team is a form of cross-functional management team and may include design, quality and manufacturing engineers as well as members from production marketing and purchasing. Products are reviewed in a phased approach to insure that all functions have input to product designs.

Project Teams

The occasion may arise when a project team is necessary on a temporary or on-going basis to develop methods of exploitation such as setup reduction or engineering changes or to study problems involved in subordination such as a quality issue and in insuring that the "necessary conditions" are being met. The project team is used to place a multitude of resources and technologies to work within the same group in solving short term problems. The project team should also be aware of how to implement effect-cause-effect, assumption models, positive as well as prerequisite trees and develop action plans so that solutions will be focused and outcomes predictable. The structure of the project team is horizontal in nature with membership being granted through appointment by the members of the cross-functional management team.

Employee Involvement (EI) Teams and Quality Circles (QC)

Employee involvement teams and quality circle groups include 3–15 shop, technical and supervisory people who meet on a regular basis to discuss problems involving exploitation and subordination as well as the requirements of the QFD program. Employees are taught the use of the elementary tools to problem solving such as statistical process control, Pareto analysis, effect-cause-effect, assumption models, positive trees, prerequisite trees and action planning. They are also taught to understand the impact of their actions in the dependent variable environment and the use of the buffer management and the control systems associated with it. EI teams as well as QC Circles may be headed by a team leader who is the foreman or line supervisor acting as a group facilitator. Additional tools may include fishbone charts, scatter diagrams and histograms.

The effectiveness of the employee involvement effort in supporting the "continuous profit improvement" program and the extent of their usefulness will depend on where the primary constraint is and whether a strategic decision has been made to support a continuous product or process improvement program. If the constraint is in the market, improving production will not improve profitability unless it is a competitive edge issue which is creating the market constraint and can be overcome through a more effective use of production. As an example, if the core cause of a market constraint is identified as a long lead time caused by production, then using the IE team to solve the lead time problem should prove an effective use of their time. If a strategic plan has been set which will require a continuous increase in quality and it can be helped through the continuous reduction of variability, then the quality circle group would be useful in supporting this effort as well. If a strategic decision is made to enter a new market segment utilizing non-constraint resources but is being blocked by a resource which is being driven to constraint levels by the proposed new forecast, then the project team or EI team could be useful in reducing the amount of load on the newly constrained resource. In facing another strategic issue, a decision to bring the constraint inside the plant must be met with a plan which considers where the new constraint will be located and what kind of support will be required from the non-constraints. The EI team and project teams are also useful during the initial implementation of TQM II.

One of the key issues of the team approach is to maximize creativity and increase communication. While the EI teams and QC Circle groups may not always be able to contribute to the overall profitability of the company and may not be as active under TQM II, the effects of communication and peer pressure should reenforce the TQM II thinking process.

ESTABLISHING FUNCTIONAL RESPONSIBILITIES

Sales and Marketing

Sales and marketing participates in the implementation of the TQM II program by:

- Determining and selling the right product mix to maximize income.
- Helping to establish multiple market segments to safeguard resources.
- Helping to set product prices using valid methods.
- Determining whether products fit customer requirements through the analysis of feedback information.
- Determining what quality characteristics will be needed to fulfill the necessary condition of good quality in the future.
- Determining the relative priority of product characteristics.
- Helping in the overall implementation of the five step improvement process
- Selling internal constraint capacity.
- Continuously examining and updating the sales and marketing policy book to eliminate policy constraints.

Manufacturing/Production

Production participates in the implementation of the TQM II process by:

- Maximizing constraint utilization through the creation of valid schedules and by supporting setup reduction, maintenance and SPC activities.
- Managing the buffer management and work improvement programs.
- Participating in design review to maximize constraint utilization and to insure proper subordination of non-constraint activities by identifying critical issues such as the clearness of design specifications, equipment requirements and hard to obtain materials.
- Participating in the development of process specifications.
- Supporting worker and process certification functions.
- Producing to specification and schedule.
- Helping in the overall implementation of the five step improvement process.
- Developing and executing the manufacturing/production management function.
- Continuously monitoring and updating the manufacturing/production policy manual to eliminate policy constraints.

Engineering

Engineering participates in the implementation of the TQM II process by:

- Developing products which meet current and future requirements for reliability, maintainability, performance, produceability and testability.

- Supporting project team activities for improving constraint utilization and for maintaining proper subordination of non-constraint activities.
- Participating in the supplier certification program.
- Participating in relevant market segmentation programs.
- Participating in design review activities.
- Helping in the overall implementation of the five step improvement process.
- Developing and executing the engineering management function.
- Continuously monitoring and updating the engineering policy manual to eliminate policy constraints.

Finance and Accounting

Finance and Accounting participates in the implementation of the TQM II process by:

- Participating in the supplier certification program.
- Administering the Throughput justification program.
- Helping in the overall implementation of the five step improvement process.
- Developing and executing the finance and accounting management function.
- Continuously monitoring and updating the finance and accounting policy manual to eliminate policy constraints.

Customer Service

Customer service participates in the implementation of the TQM II process by:

- Helping to establish multiple market segments to safeguard resources.
- Helping to determine whether products fit customer requirements through the analysis of feed-back information.
- Helping to determine what quality characteristics will be needed to fulfill the necessary condition of good quality in the future.
- Helping to determine the relative priority of product characteristics.
- Helping in the overall implementation of the five step improvement process.
- Participating in the design review process.
- Developing and executing the customer service management function.
- Continuously examining and updating the customer service policy book to eliminate policy constraints.

Quality Assurance

Quality assurance participates in the implementation of the TQM II process by:

- Offering training and consulting services for insuring the availability of qualified employees and for maintaining trouble free processes.
- Participating in relevant customer relations programs.

- Administering the audit and survey programs.
- Managing the metrology program.
- Administering the inspection and test programs.
- Participating in the design review process to insure proper subordination of the quality activity.
- Participating in the supplier certification program.
- Helping to set and administer the continuous product improvement strategy.
- Establishing and maintaining the process capability program.
- Establishing and maintaining the statistical process control program.
- Helping in the overall implementation of the five step improvement process.
- Developing and executing the quality assurance management function.
- Continuously examining and updating the quality assurance policy book to eliminate policy constraints.

DOCUMENTATION

The next task in creating the TQM II management system is to insure that a well established system of documentation exists which is designed to support those activities required to fulfill the "necessary condition" and the implementation of the five step process for all who are involved. Specific documentation includes:

- The corporate policy manual.
- The quality assurance manual.
- The functional procedures manual.
- Process specifications manual.

The Corporate Policy Manual

The corporate policy manual defines the corporate goals and objectives and establishes guidelines for the development of corporate procedures and strategies. It outlines the importance of quality as it relates to the customer and defines the method for insuring that the customer's quality objectives are met. It also sets the stage for focusing on Throughput and managing through the five steps of "continuous profit improvement". Typical subjects covered include guidelines for:

- Marketing and the development of market segmentation strategies or methods for determining product mix.
- Engineering and methods of new product introduction.
- The role of quality assurance.
- Establishing methods of process planning and control.
- The implementation of measurement and decision processes.

A guideline example might be requiring the use of a phased approach for new product introduction which takes into consideration quality function deployment issues as well as the dependent variable environment or a statement requiring the use of Throughput, Inventory and Operating Expense as the basic measurement system. Special interest is given during the implementation process to changing the corporate policy manual to include the new methods of focus and operation.

Typical policy statements include:

- Quality is to be viewed as a necessary condition and is to be supported by the Quality Function Deployment process.
- Establishing a program to support "continuous profit improvement" will be the rule and will be pursued by all functions.
- Throughput, Inventory and Operating Expense are the measurements of choice and will be adopted for use by all functions and incorporated into the decision process.
- The necessary level of quality is to be built in not inspected into the product.
- TQM II will be a key consideration in source selection, and vendors will be treated as partners.
- TQM II concepts and practices are to be ingrained throughout the company through tailored, continuous, lifelong, training for everyone; starting with top management.
- Dedicated, competent, and involved employees will be recognized and rewarded appropriately.

The Quality Assurance Manual

The quality assurance manual documents the quality plan to include procedures for:

- Inspection and test to establish the relationship between the products being produced and the QFD requirements, and to support the subordination process.
- Audits and surveys to give feedback to managers of the overall effectiveness of the management systems, the degree to which they follow corporate guidelines and whether they are being followed.
- The metrology program to develop and regulate testing devices.
- Non-conforming material disposition to determine whether products should be scrapped or reworked.
- The overall statistical methods program to include the type of methods to be used and where and how they are to be focused.
- New product planning to insure that the customers needs are fulfilled and that the limitations and opportunities provided by the environment are not overlooked.
- Supplier relations to insure that products and services provided by vendors meet with established guidelines for product quality.
- The subordination of the quality process.

- Establishing feedback mechanisms such as next process inspection and failsafing devices.
- Determining where and how to focus variance reduction programs.

The Procedures Manual

Describes the responsibilities and method of operation for each functional organization within the company. Specific interest is given to insuring that each function has a well documented method of determining how to best exploit or subordinate to the constraint and to determine what actions are required to meet the necessary condition of good quality.

It documents the decision processes to be used and measurement systems supported. Included in the procedures manual are instructions for programs such as:

- The implementation of the maintenance, setup reduction and variation control programs.
- The day to day operation of materials management, sales and marketing, engineering, and finance and accounting.
- Methods of scheduling and controlling the shop floor.
- Instructions for managing employees and conducting employee involvement programs.

The Process Specifications Manual

The process specifications manual is the results of converting product specifications into process specifications within the QFD program and is the mechanism by which the process requirements are relayed to individuals within each process. It contains detailed instructions and tolerance information so that workers can accomplish the task of production. Included in the manual are instructions for assembly, fabrication and machining as well as the acceptable limitations. Typical process specification manuals for a printed circuit board manufacturer might contain pictures of how an acceptable or unacceptable solder joint looks. In preparing the process specifications the preparer should avoid presenting vague information requiring unnecessary interpretation by the operator. He should cover thoroughly the important product characteristics and explain why a certain process is to be completed in a certain manner or why a certain specification has been set.

FEEDBACK AND CONTROL MECHANISMS

Feedback and control mechanisms are designed to relay information about a systems performance from a local as well as global perspective and to offer possible alternatives or enforce correction. It is at the heart of the basic TQM program and holds a similar position within TQM II. TQM II offers a focusing mechanism for determining where and how to implement the old methods such as murphy proofing, self inspection, next process inspection and statistical methods but also has some unique methods for setting priorities and determining global impact.

The Concept of Source Inspection

Source inspection is an important ingredient in the overall TQM process. Conceptually, the emphasis is on inspecting and correcting problems as close to the object process as possible. Operator feedback is immediate, inspection levels reach 100% without additional operating expense, and social pressures require performance.

Note: While the general trend is to move away from source inspection by designing better processes and products, the need for source inspection will carry on until the time arrives when it can be eliminated.

Failsafing devices (categorized by purpose and method) prevent defects from occurring: control devices prevent defects and warning devices give notice of pending defects. A machine modified to allow a part to be installed only one way is a control device; a buzzer which sounds when a defect is about to occur is a warning device. Failsafing devices include pressure-sensitive switches, thermometers, electrical current sensors, light-activated switches, and counters.

Self inspection utilizes checklists for operators to insure that certain critical operations were done correctly. Operators inspect their own work after the process is completed.

Next process inspection uses the next person in the process to inspect the work of the previous process. Discovered defects result in the work being returned immediately to the causing departments or operations.

Statistical Process Control

In statistical process control (SPC) the emphasis is on continuous process monitoring; the assumption is that a process under control will yield acceptable product. The operator establishes the average value and range of deviations from the mean in a process and plots those values in the form of X-Bar and R charts (figure 8.1).

Pre-control limits are set and sample measurements are taken from the products being produced. The operator then monitors the outcome of each plot or group of plots to determine if a trend is developing or if the process is out of control. If it is out of control, the process is stopped, the cause determined and a solution implemented. (See chapter ten on Statistical Process Control).

Pre-control, a simplified version of SPC, focuses more on process control/capability verification and less on charting (figure 8.2).

Pre-control process lines (PC lines) are set in the middle half of the product specification width. Process capabilities are established at the beginning of production by measuring five consecutive occurrences, each of which must appear in the green zone. Periodic sampling indicates whether the process is under control. (The frequency of sampling is determined by dividing the time interval between failures

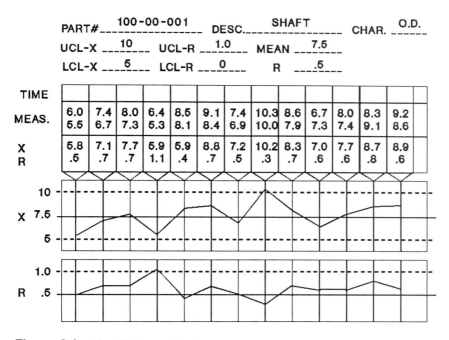

Figure 8.1 The X-Bar and R chart.

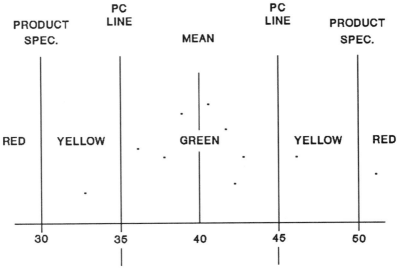

Figure 8.2   Pre-control.

by six.) Two units are measured during each sample, and the process is stopped if two measurements are in the yellow zone or one is in the red.
(Portions of the above information on source inspection were printed with permission, the American Production and Inventory Control Society, *Production and Inventory Management Journal*, Vol. 32, No. 1, (1991), pp. 7.)

Since source inspections provide immediate feedback these type of mechanisms are excellent for monitoring the most critical portions of the factory which need to react quickly to problems which impact Throughput, to include:

- Primary and secondary constraint(s).
- Resources which feed the constraint directly.
- The chain of resources leading from the constraint to the sales order.
- Those resources designated as critical to the QFD program.

Buffer Management

Buffer management provides information on the success of the overall program from a global perspective by aggregating the impact of problems which will effect the buffer origin and provides a roadmap for corrections as seen earlier. Also seen earlier, the implementation of Throughput Dollar Days and Inventory Dollar Days as control measurements forces action from offending resources to make corrections.

Audits and Surveys

Audits and surveys were originally designed to provide an indication to management of the effectiveness of the overall system. They concentrated on whether procedures had been put into place which would gain the proper result and whether or not these procedures were being followed. Key issues included laws and regulations, employee and customer safety, and conformance to specification. Of prime importance was determining whether or not proper decision mechanisms and measurements were being used. There is a warning that must be given with regard to the effectiveness of the audit/survey program. Audits and surveys look at a broad spectrum and tend to widen the overall focus of management. Since very few things must change to support the process of "continuous profit improvement", in reacting to fix those things found in the audit or survey by spending money, profitability may actually decline. The focused approach of using the effect-cause-effect, assumption modeling and positive as well as prerequisite trees will identify what needs to be changed and how to accomplish it in far less time. Audits and surveys should be used sparingly to gain an overall view as to the validity of decision processes and procedures being used and whether they are being followed. The objective would be to get an indication of what problems may surface in the future.

Inspection and Test

The inspection and test process refers to the process of determining whether a product's characteristics conform to specification, and then making a disposition and recording the data. It is usually performed by a group outside of the production organization. Under TQM II the basic concept of inspection and test has not changed from traditional TQM. Inspection and test is still the method of last resort because of the length of the delay in feedback to the offending operation. However, there are still times when a more detailed procedure is needed by qualified people to insure product compliance.

Like source inspection the method of focusing the inspection and test process has changed to comply with the QFD program and the realities dictated by the dependent variable environment.

Benchmarking

Benchmarking has been described as making a comparison of how well one corporation is performing in relation with another. Similar operations are compared to determine whether improvement is available or should be warranted and to determine what, if anything can be done to improve. The usual benchmarking endeavor includes comparing cycle times or reject rates for similar operations.

There is danger in this process. What is being used is a correlative approach. Since most corporations will differ as to where the constraint is, any comparison might prove useless. Unless both companies had the constraint located in the same resource and were determined to exploit and subordinate in the same fashion, there may be no similarities to compare. Each company would be attempting to maximize different processes.

The net effect would probably be that improvements would be made in the wrong places. If money was spent, profitability would decline.

Companies seeking to benchmark should be very specific in what they are looking for. The objective is to maximize profitability not improve every resource. It might be interesting to see how other companies have exploited similar constraint or near constraint resources, to look at methods of subordination and to see how product presence in the market might compare between competitors.

Process Certification Program

Process certification is designed to insure that a process is capable of consistently producing to specification and to insure that each resource understands its role in the exploitation and subordination process. The certification of a process includes insuring that:

- The proper documentation is available.
- People have been properly trained and are performing to process specification and documentation.
- Test equipment and tools are available and the calibration program is in place.
- Workmanship standards are released.
- Inspection criteria have been determined and inspectors prepared.
- Process capability studies have been completed and the process is found capable.
- Process controls are in place and functioning.
- Employees are capable of making valid decisions in support of exploitation and subordination.

Workers who do not understand the impact of their decisions or are unable to make decisions from a global perspective will not be able to perform.

Summary

The TQM II Infrastructure will have a significant impact on the overall implementation of TQM II by creating a structure and acting to formalize the process. It enhances communication at a management as well as operational level and insures that action will be taken to solve problems. It serves to immediately indoctrinate new employees into the process and provides adequate documentation for them to learn what is expected of them and how they fit into the overall program.

9

Product/Process Design

This chapter introduces key issues associated with the design process and establishes a platform for designing products which will meet the necessary conditions of good quality and at the same time will support the process of continuous profit improvement.

OBJECTIVES

- To create the process for converting customer requirements into product/process designs so that the necessary conditions of good quality can be met.
- To insure that the design process properly supports the exploitation, subordination and elevation phases of the process of continuous profit improvement.

DEFINING THE DESIGN FUNCTION

The function of product/process design is to convert customer needs into product/process specifications. How well a company can accomplish this task, in many cases, will determine whether or not it will continue to meet the necessary condition of good quality and remain as a profitable entity. Those companies failing to continually meet the requirements of the customer will soon become extinct. It is necessary then to understand what it is the customer wants or needs and then be able to convert these wants and desires into instructions for those who must perform the act of creating the product or performing the service. It is also desirable to do so in a way which will maximize the profitability of the company.

QUALITY FUNCTION DEPLOYMENT (QFD)

Product quality is defined as delivering what the customer wanted, on time and free of defects. To be effective, a quality program should be able to recognize when a product is perceived as no longer adequate in the customers eyes now and to be able to predict when it will be inadequate in the future, so that corrections can be made. All efforts should be made to insure that the customer's perception of the quality of goods and services it receives is at least equal to the competition so that it can be prevented from becoming the constraint to making more money. To do this means that the customers current and future desires and perceptions as well as the degree to which the competition is satisfying them currently and an estimate of how well the competition will be satisfying them in the future, must be known. Once an understanding of the customers needs has been developed, in order to meet those requirements, each function must understand what part it plays in fulfilling the customers needs.

The Quality Function Deployment (QFD) program creates an organizational structure and control method for managing the coordinated development of products and services based on customer demand. It assigns product or process characteristics which are desirable to meet the demand and identifies those functions/ organizations and activities necessary. Emphasis is placed on the use of the Seven New Management Planning Tools to obtain better product definition, communication and documentation during the design process so that design/redesign times are held to a minimum. In addition, the QFD program compares those requirements to how well the competition is meeting them.

PLANNING FOR TOTAL QUALITY MANAGEMENT (THE SEVEN NEW TOOLS)

One of the problems inherent in the Shewhart planning cycle of plan-do-check-action is trying to determine what to plan. The Management Planning tool concept uses an intricate system of tools which are designed to create a detailed understanding of complex problems and to capitalize on the creative abilities of managers and employees in investigating and solving them so that effective plans can be created and executed. It begins with an assimilation of data into correlative and logical structures, and ends with a process for scheduling and controlling the implementation plan. These tools include:

- The Affinity Diagram.
- The Relations Diagram.
- The Tree Diagram.
- The Matrix Diagram.
- The Matrix Data Analysis Chart.
- The Process Decision Program Chart.
- The Arrow Diagram.

Each tool fulfills a specific role in the overall planning process and are used in a group forum to facilitate a group accepted solution and a wider understanding of the issues involved.

Affinity Diagram

The Affinity Diagram is an intuitive process for developing ideas and examining complex issues which uses brainstorming and cards to organize input from various sources. To create the Affinity Diagram the following steps should be used:

- Select a group of people with a common interests and familiarity about the subject to be examined. Assemble them and give each member a stack of cards.
- State the issue to be examined and give the group 10 minutes to respond by writing one idea on each card. Members should avoid communication.
- After ten minutes each member in succession will read one idea and place it on the table in front of them. There should be no discussion of ideas at this time. New ideas generated during this process should also be written down and presented.
- After all ideas have been generated the cards should be arranged in related stacks and a common label selected for each stack.

Figure 9.1 illustrates.

The objective of the Affinity diagram is to maximize the number of ideas being generated and then to categorize them for further examination.

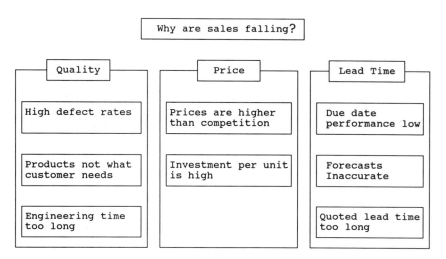

Figure 9.1   The Affinity diagram.

Relations Diagram

When studying complex issues it is often necessary to look for relationships and patterns to begin to develop so that they can be better understood. The Relationship Diagram is a logical method for exploring relationships between factors. It is commonly used in conjunction with those ideas and concepts developed in the Affinity diagramming process, although it is not a requirement. A central idea, concept or problem is presented and then all the logical connections to these issues are determined. The logical connections can sometimes go through numerous levels before a complete picture of all the relationships involved are discovered. Each level may be a prerequisite for determining the relationship of the next. The two major uses of this method include multiple and single level problem solving and can be effective in addressing quality, management policies, production issues and design problems. To create the Relationship Diagram the following steps are used:

- Select and assemble a group of people with a common interests and familiarity about the subject to be examined. This will probably be the same group used during the Affinity diagramming process. (Note: It may be appropriate for the group facilitator to have attempted creating the diagram on the same subject independent of the group so that process time can be minimized).
- Select and define the central issue to be examined and write this on a card or on a black or dry erase board to be displayed in a central location.
- Brainstorm for ideas on cause or prerequisite relationships writing each concept or idea on the board in the proximity of the central issue. Add arrows to build a picture of the relationships of ideas. Repeat the process for new ideas as they are developed to create a broad picture of all relationships and to look for major issues and root causes to be examined more closely.

Figure 9.2 illustrates a completed Relationship Diagram where the objective of the exercise was to determine the relationship of the batching, material and resource utilization policies on the competitive edge issues of quality, lead time, and price.

Each concept may be better distinguished from others through the use of boxes or circles. A double box or circle is used to set aside key problems or issues. In this case bold type has been used.

The Tree Diagram

Is a methodical process for describing the stepped activity necessary for achieving the desired goal. It to is a group activity and maps individual prerequisites which must be performed in order to accomplish a specific goal. To create the Tree Diagram the following steps should be used:

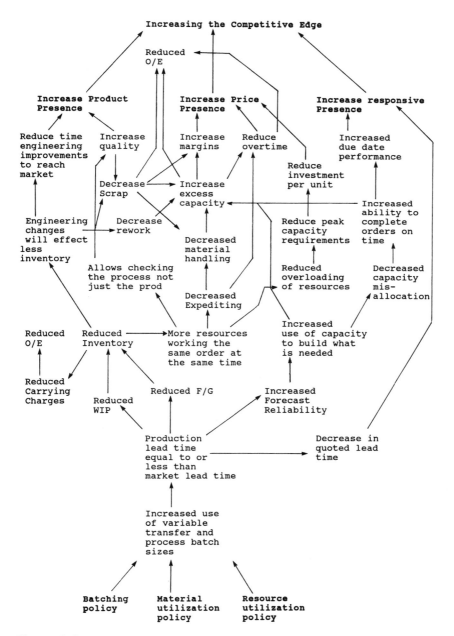

Figure 9.2 The Relations diagram.

- The first step is to adequately identify the goal to be accomplished. It is very important to understand precisely what the goal is. As in the Relationship Diagram cards or a black board may be used during the process to record ideas and to communicate.
- In open forum determine what the prerequisites are to accomplishing the goal and write them next to or under the goal with arrows or lines leading to the goal. Ask the question "what must be done or what is the prerequisite to accomplishing the goal".
- Once the first set of prerequisites have been finished the next can begin. Starting with one of the prerequisites to the goal determine what its prerequisites might be.

This process is repeated until all prerequisites have been discovered and becomes the basis of an action plan for accomplishing the goal. Figure 9.3 illustrates.

The Matrix Diagram

The Matrix Diagram was designed to establish the extent of relationships or the degree of correlation between 2 sets of data such as:

- Tasks to be performed and the people or functions which must perform them.
- Effects which exist in the environment and contributing causes.
- Specific customer requirements and design requirements.

The Matrix Diagram can take many forms. However, the most commonly used is the L shaped diagram where one set of data is presented on the x axis and another is presented on the y axis. The correlation is determined at the point of intersection. Figure 9.4 illustrates the use of the Matrix Diagram in assigning responsibility for prerequisites developed in figure 9.3 (Tree Diagram).

One of the primary functions of the Matrix Diagram is at the very heart of Quality Function Deployment. The process begins with an analysis of customer demand and proceeds through a series of succeeding matrix diagrams until the product and all its requirements have been fully described. Brainstorming sessions are used to aid in the process. Each matrix is used as input for the next in a cascading fashion which includes requirements for customers, product designs, product characteristics, manufacturing/purchasing, and control/verification. See figure 9.5.

In figure 9.6 customer requirements are converted to design requirements and passed on to the next level which details the engineering design requirements.

For a more definitive explanation of requirements each level may be broken down into primary, secondary and tertiary requirements. See figure 9.7.

A coding system is used to detail the relative importance of specific relationships between the requirements at one level and the requirements at the next level down in the flow. See figure 9.8.

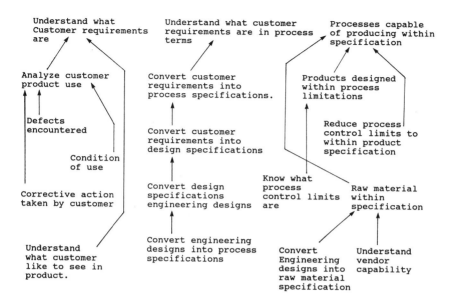

Figure 9.3 The Tree diagram. (Goals: have processes capable of meeting customer requirements).

The relative importance of correlations are also established between requirements at the same level. See figure 9.9.

The objective of the weighting system is to give relative priority to supporting activities and to establish the level of effort required.

Additional information is added such as customer evaluations of competitive products, benchmarks, the degree of technical difficulty, the relative values of each design requirement in meeting the objective and the target values established during the engineering process. This process results in a total view of the relative quality of products and the priorities and technical difficulties associated with the project (figure 9.10).

Improving the QFD Process

Originally included in the QFD process described by John R. Hauser and Don Clausing, in a Harvard Business Review article published in the May-June 1988 issue entitled The House of Quality were provisions for including an estimation of relative cost in percentage terms for each level in the process. As this would serve to distort the design process another method must be found.

Function

P - Primary Responsibility C - Contributor Tasks	Design Eng	Manuf Eng	Quality	Production	Purchasing	Marketing	Cust. Serv
Analyze customer product use	C		C			P	P
Understand what customer wants	C					P	P
Convert cust requirement to design specifications	P		C	C		C	C
Convert design specs to engineering designs	P						
Convert engineering designs to process specs	P	P	C	C			
Provide process control limit information				P	P		
Design product w/in process control limits	P	C	C	C			
Reduce process variation to within product spec				P	P		
Convert eng. designs into raw material specs	P	C					
Understand vendor capability	C	C	C	C	P		

Figure 9.4 The Matrix diagram.

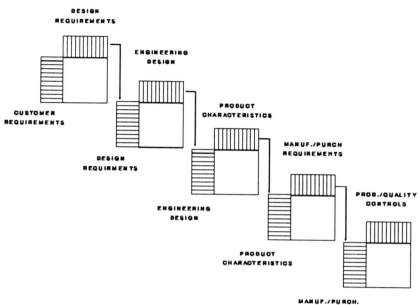

Figure 9.5 The QFD Matrix.

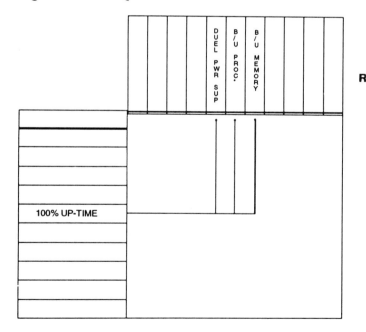

CUSTOMER

REQUIREMENTS

Figure 9.6 The Design Matrix.

PRIMARY	SECONDARY	TERTIARY

Figure 9.7 Using primary, secondary and tertiary definitions.

⊙ VERY STRONG RELATIONSHIP

○ STRONG RELATIONSHIP

△ WEAK RELATIONSHIP

PRIMARY	SECONDARY	TERTIARY								
			○	○	○	○	○	○	⊙	○
			○	⊙		△	△	⊙		○
			⊙	△	⊙	△	⊙	○	○	○
			⊙	△	△	⊙		△		
			⊙	△			○			○
			△	⊙		⊙		○	△	△
					⊙				○	

Figure 9.8 Attaching relative importance.

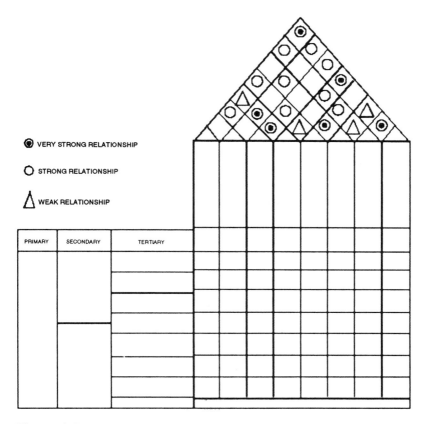

Figure 9.9 Comparing importance at the same level.

It is suggested that a better understanding from a global perspective can be obtained by attempting to understand the impact of certain design requirements or product characteristics on the three measurements of Throughput, Inventory and Operating Expense. Some ensight is given to this process later in this chapter in the section on constraint exploitation. However, at issue is whether or not this kind of data can be included in the QFD process without distorting the relative importance of each characteristic from a global perspective.

Two measurements which may be tried within the House of Quality Matrix is the relative cost of raw material and the degree of constraint absorption. Since minimizing each during the design process will result in more money coming into the company it may prove to be an effective mechanism. This would require two additional lines be added underneath target values in figure 9.10. Each characteristic would be gaged based on its relative impact to the constraint and total raw material cost in percentage terms.

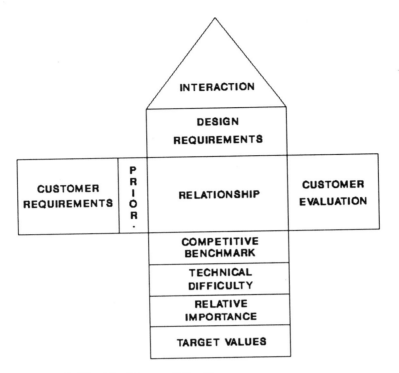

Figure 9.10 The House of Quality.

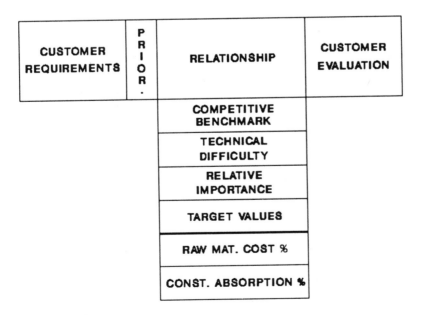

Note: There are some problems in using this method which concerns the aggregation of demand and will be discussed later in more detail.

Other matrixes not included in this brief discussion are T type for relating two sets of data to a third, C type for correlating three data sets to an intersection point, the Y type for comparing three data sets to each other and X type for correlating four data sets.

The Matrix Data Analysis Chart

The Matrix Data Analysis Chart is used for establishing the significants of relationships between variables and is used extensively in marketing research. A simple version may compare different types of products to desirable attributes so that a visible comparison can be made between competitive products. In the following example the attributes of Great Taste and Less Filling appear on the x and y axis. Various customers would be asked to compare each beer against the two attributes. Each beer is coded to prevent bias.

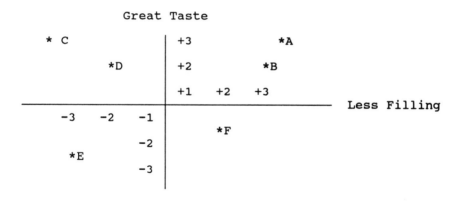

This type of information would be used to create a marketing or quality improvement plan for one of the beer companies.

The Process Decision Program Chart (PDPC)

The Process Decision Program Chart supports the creation of solutions through an analysis of possible alternatives. Like the tree diagram it is a methodical and detailed approach to the thinking process. It begins with a problem or possible solution and attempts to predict the outcome. Unlike the tree diagram where the question being asked is "what is the prerequisite" the PDPC asks "what is the possible outcome or problem". To create the Process Decision Program Chart the following steps are used:

- Begin with a problem statement or possible problem solution. The Tree and Relations Diagrams are excellent sources.
- Ask the question "What is the possible outcome or problem?".

- After establishing an initial outcome continue asking the same question until each branch has been completed.
- Whenever a problem is encountered within a branch, countermeasures for overcoming the problem may be listed out to one side or below. Each countermeasure may be the subject of a separate PDPC.
- Select the next problem or possible solution and continue the process.

PDPC is excellent for use in areas where there is no experiential information available or for developing Failure Mode, Effects and Criticality Analysis information. Figure 9.11 illustrates:

The Arrow Diagram

The Arrow Diagram is used for determining and scheduling subordinate activities much like the Program Evaluation and Review Technique (PERT) or the Critical Path Method (CPM). It can be used in conjunction with projects such as product design or construction. The following symbols are used.

- Arrows indicate the direction of flow of a task from one node to another and the relative length of time required to perform.
- Nodes are indicated with circles and represent the starting or finishing of a task.
- Each node is numbered to indicate what node is represented and in what order it is placed.

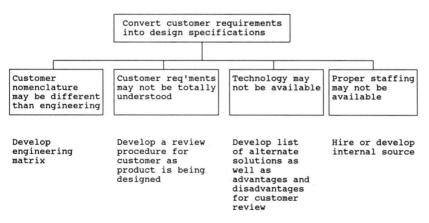

Figure 9.11   The Process Decision Program Chart.

- Dotted lines indicate connections between nodes but have no time associated with them.
- To create the Arrow Diagram the following steps are used:
- Determine all necessary tasks to be performed and write each task on a separate card.
- Determine which tasks/cards proceed or are performed in conjunction with other tasks/cards and place them in sequence.
- Locate those cards which, when placed in a series, form the longest chain and lay them out end to end. This will be used to judge the relative position of all other cards.
- Locate all parallel paths placing them in relative position.
- Begin numbering each card in sequence and estimate the time required to perform each task.
- Establish the relative length for measuring time and begin placing nodes, arrows and dotted lines on the medium used to present the diagram. Add the numbers for each node.

By using arrows with a relative time associated with length, the critical path will be generated automatically. The Time Earliest (T/E), the earliest time that a process can begin or end, is determined by adding the time associated with each arrow, in succession, to the time for the previous node, beginning with the first node. The Time Earliest (T/E) for the first node is time zero. The Time Earliest (T/E) for the second node, in this case, is time zero plus 5. Figure 9.12 illustrates.

To determine the Time Latest (T/L), the latest time a process can begin or end, can be determined by starting at the last node, in this case node 6, and working backwards by subtracting the time required for the intervening arrow. When dealing with the critical path the Time Earliest (T/E) and Time Latest (T/L) will be the same. However, for those nodes not lying on the critical path the time latest will be different. Figure 9.13 illustrates.

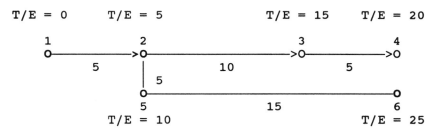

Figure 9.12   The Arrow diagram.

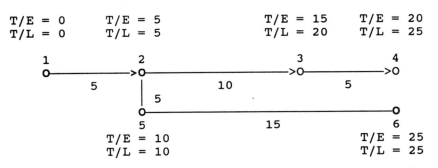

Figure 9.13   Establishing time latest and time earliest.

The amount of "slack time", or allowable delay for any operation which can occur before jeopardizing the project's due date, is determined by subtracting the time earliest from the time latest.

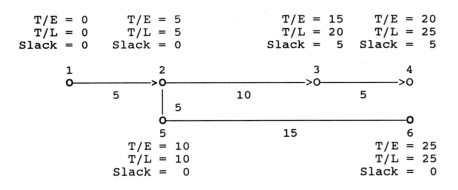

In this case the slack time for operations 3 and 4 is 5 days. The slack time for the critical path is zero.

Problems With the Arrow Diagram

The Arrow Diagram for scheduling projects may create more problems than it solves and may actually result in the extension of projects well beyond requirements. These problems include:

• Like Material Requirements Planning, the Arrow Diagram is capacity insensitive and only reacts to the order in which events should occur.
• It does not take into consideration the way in which resources interact nor does it attempt to shorten lead times through maximizing the use of parallel operations.

- Since it is capacity insensitive it cannot judge whether or not a constraint exists nor the extent of protective or excess capacity available.
- Lead times are the result of the impact of the load on a specific resource or group of resources and cannot be predetermined. They are dynamic and yet the lead times used in the Arrow Diagram are stagnant. To determine lead times a schedule should first be built.
- Additional time allotted for "Murphy" is spread throughout the project and cannot be judged based on its global impact.

It has been suggested that a better method of scheduling projects would be the DBR process discussed in chapter six. Since it is based on a concept of the dynamics involved with interacting resources and dependent variables it should be more effective in creating a valid schedule for maximizing Throughput. Care should be taken to insure that a maximum of operations are run in parallel whenever possible.

Additional Issues

When addressing planning issues and attempting to solve problems one of the biggest issues faced is to insure that core problems are addressed and not just the symptoms. Within the QFD umbrella the Affinity Diagram, Relations Diagram and Matrix Diagrams are excellent for creating correlations between data and for methodically analyzing complex issues. However, what is also needed is a method which will increase the probability that core problems will be uncovered and solved. Many times relationships between activities are assumed but in fact may not exist. Under TQM II whether dealing with satisfying the "necessary condition" or supporting the process of "continuous profit improvement", the Effect-Cause-Effect method increases the probability that core problems will be addressed by substantiating the supposed cause with an additional effect. Working somewhat like a tree diagram instead of asking for prerequisites it asks the question "why" an effect exists. A supposed cause is then theorized which should be supported by an additional effect. See Chapter four on analyzing policy constraints.

Additionally, during the design process, decisions between two alternatives and whether or not to maximize any given part specification must be examined from more than just the customer's perspective. Chapter eleven on Implementing SPC for Quality and Profit includes the alternatives of scrap or rework on the Throughput of the company. These same type of issues will apply to the implementation of QFD at the resource level.

Failure Mode, Effects and Criticality Analysis (FMECA)

Failure mode, effects and criticality analysis is the methodical study of proposed product designs for possible failure conditions and their impacts on the overall system and subsystems of products (Juran, 1988). The objective is to determine what product features are critical to a given mode of failure and to determine its effects and what the possible solutions might be. Design efforts can then be focused on the most critical portion of the design based on the level of criticality. Critical components effect product safety, mission goals, manufacturability and maintainability.

Block diagrams or tables are used to track the various cause and effect relationships throughout the product and to indicate criticality and suggest alternatives. See figure 9.14.

The impact of the failure is given a rating from one to ten based on the probability of occurrence, the seriousness of the results and how easy it would be to detect. A rating of one in each category would indicate that the problem was not serious, that the probability of occurrence would be low, or that the detectability would be high. A ten in each category would indicate that the particular feature needs serious consideration for redesign.

```
                    1  .   .  .   5  .   .   .   .   10
Probability        Low                          High

Seriousness        Low                          High

Detectability      High                         Low
```

The criticality index is determined for each failure mode by multiplying the rating for each category of impact.

```
Probability  X  Seriousness  X  Detectability  =  Index
```

Product/ Feature	Failure Mode	Failure Effect	Failure Cause	Impact P S D	Possible Solutions
Tail Rotor Drive Shaft	Out of Balance	Med Speed Vibration	Loss of Balance Weight	5 5 2	Pre-Flight/ Maint/In- Flight Test Change Epoxy
	Loose Mounts	Med Speed Vibration	Metal Fatigue	3 9 2	Pre-Flight/ Maintenance Inspections Harden Mount
	Worn Bearings	Med Speed Vibration	Metal Fatigue	4 9 5	Pre-Flight/ Maintenance Inspections Harden Bearing

Figure 9.14 Failure Mode Effects and Criticality Analysis.

The resulting index scores are then listed from highest to lowest to determine the order of priority. For the failure modes listed above the index would be:

Failure Mode	Failure Effect	Failure Cause	Rating
Worn Bearings	Med Speed Vibration	Metal Fatigue	180
Loose Mounts	Med Speed Vibration	Metal Fatigue	54
Out of Balance	Med Speed Vibration	Loss of Balance Weight	50

Analysis of Reliability

The objective of reliability analysis is to predict the reliability of a system (Juran, 1988). There are two issues:

- The impact of time.
- The cumulative impact of component dependence.

In analyzing the impact of time, the objective is to determine the probability for a product's functioning at specific points in time. The formula for product reliability at a specific point in time is.

$$\text{Reliability (t)} = \frac{\text{The number surviving at time (t)}}{\text{Total number}}$$

If a total of 100 parts had been created and 70 were still functioning 12 months later. Reliability at 12 months would be:

$$R(12) = \frac{70}{100} = 70\%$$

Reliability over time usually follows a predictable pattern where products fail at an increasing rate at the beginning and end of their normal life cycles. The early stage is usually referred to as the "infant mortality stage" where the latest stage is referred to as the "wear out stage". The period in between is the "adult stage".

In predicting system reliability the interdependence of components must be considered. Each component is rated for individual reliability and then the impact of using these components together is determined by multiplying successive reliability ratings together.

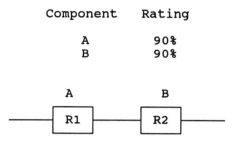

```
Component    Rating

    A          90%
    B          90%
```

```
Reliability  =  R1  X  R2
Reliability  =  .90  X  .90  =  .81 or 81%
```

The individual rating for electronic components A and B are set at 90%. However, when these components are used together in a circuit the rating would be 81% reliability.

Reliability can be increased by using redundancy where more than one part or group of parts performs the same function.

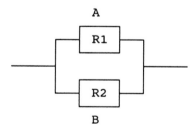

In this case parts A and B form a redundant circuit. The reliability for the circuit would be:

```
Reliability  =  1-(1-R1)(1-R2)

Reliability  =  1-(1-.90)(1-.90)  =  .99 or 99%
```

Individual component reliability may be expressed in ways other than percentage form such as failures per thousand hours of use. In which case the circuit would also be described in failure per thousand hours of use.

Designing for Maintainability

In manufacturing the importance of process maintainability is impacted by the way in which resources interface and is a question of the required availability to perform the mission. Availability is described as a function of mean time between failure (MTBF) and mean time to repair (MTTR). However, maintainability from a design perspective is generally customer driven and is more of a question of:

- The allowable mean time to repair (MTTR).
- The probability that repair will be executed within the allowable downtime.

Maintainability prediction assumes that MTTR is predictable much the same as reliability and as such institutes a program for establishing component down time probability and then extending to develop an overall system for mean time to repair predictions. Repair time historical information is gathered for like components of previous products and is assigned to current product designs. Once complete, when compared with QFD requirements on availability and reliability a clear picture on where improvements must take place will develop. Based on historical data a probability for repairing the product within certain time parameters can also be developed.

Phased Development

- Feasibility—During the feasibility phase a determination of whether the product can be designed and manufactured to customer need and what the future impact will be on Throughput, Inventory and Operating Expense.
- Design—During the design phase various alternative designs are reviewed and a primary candidate selected. Key issues include raw material availability and cost, the impact on internal resources, and expected reliability and maintainability. Specifications are prepared in enough detail to create the prototype.
- Prototype—In the prototype phase the product is built and tested to specification. Prototyping should accomplish two tasks; to test the design to see if the product performs as expected and to test the feasibility of manufacture.
- Pre-production—An additional, more advanced prototyping may need to be accomplished to iron out the details of full scale production. The pre-production phase is used to "hand off" the product from design engineering to production. Manufacturing engineers review product designs as well as the prototypes to determine the best method of manufacture and request design changes, if necessary, to enhance manufacturability. Key issues include; standardization of materials, degree of constraint absorption and fixture requirements, etc.
- Production—This phase represents full production and delivery to the customer. Special care is made to insure that initial full production problems are addressed.

An additional phase is sometimes added for post production design review to insure continued manufacturability and to suggest product improvements.

Design Review

Each phase of development is accompanied by a design review. The design review team insures that a wide variety of expertise is available to review each phase of design so that the problems which normally accompany the introduction of a new product are minimized. The design review team should insure that designs are reviewed well ahead of the production release date and that each meeting is well planned so that documentation is available. Checklists are usually used for the organization of the meeting so that all aspects of the product are reviewed. Special care must be given to creating a non-threatening atmosphere for the review. It should be a positive meeting rather than viewed as a chance to "hang the designer". Figure 9.15 is a modification of the design review team membership and responsibility chart taken from Juran's Quality Control Handbook (1988) and outlines individual design team members and their responsibilities. Special consideration was given to certain issues of invalid cost management as well as to the impact of the design process on the dependent variable environment and the overall profitability of the company. Asterisks indicate modifications.

Every member of the design review team must be keenly aware of what actions are necessary in the design process to insure the overall profitability of the company and what the impact of their actions are on the dependent variable environment.

Exploiting the Constraint

Perhaps the largest contributor to product quality is the concept of the manufacturability of design. Factors having a direct effect on manufacturability include:

- Number of Parts (minimize).
- Variability of Components (minimize).
- Process Requirements (simplify).
- Degree of Design Detail (simplify).
- Technology Employed (should be proven).
- Availability of Materials (high).
- Degree of Production Involvement (high).
- Design for Yield (within process capabilities).

(The above factors were printed with permission, the American Production and Inventory Control Society, *Production and Inventory Management Journal,* Vol. 32, No. 1, (1991), pp. 7.)

While these are excellent guidelines for the design process in preventing problems from occurring and can themselves create constraints if not given the proper

Member	Responsibility
Chairperson	Calls, conducts meetings of group, and issues interim and final reports.
Design Engineer	Prepares and presents designs and substantiates decisions with data from tests or calculations.
Reliability Engineer	Evaluates design for optimum reliability consistent with goals.
Quality Engineer	Insures that the functions of inspection, control, and test can be effectively carried out.
Manufacturing * Engineer	Insures that designs are produceable, reviews the impact new designs will have on internal resource constraints/non-constraints, that constraint utilization is minimized where possible and that subordination can be properly accomplished.
Field engineer	Insures that installation, maintenance, and user considerations were included in the design.
Purchasing	Insures that acceptable parts and materials are available to meet cost and delivery schedules.
Materials Engineer	Insures that materials selected will perform as required.
Tooling * Engineer	Evaluates design in terms of the tooling impact on T, I & O/E as well as tolerance and functional requirements. Special consideration is given to the overall impact of the new design on the dependent variable issues. As an Example, should a new tool be created which will reduce the impact the new product will have on the constraint and therefore increase the Throughput created per unit of the constraint.
Packaging and Shipping Engineer	Assures that the product can be safely handled without damage.
Marketing * Representative	Assures that requirements of customers are realistic and fully understood by all parties. The marketing rep. is also there to understand the impact the new product will have on current marketing strategies. As an Example, will the new product change the location of the constraint and therefore the pricing, product mix and marketing segmentation strategies and, if so, how.
Design Engineer (not associated with product under review)	Constructively reviews adequacy of design to meet all requirements of customer.
Consultants, * specialists on components, value, human factors etc.	Evaluates design for compliance with goals of performance, the impact on the dependent variable environment and schedule.
Customer Representative	Generally voices opinion as to the acceptability of design and may request further investigation on specific items.

Figure 9.15 The design review team. (*Source*: Juran, 1988. Asterisks indicate modification.)

amount of attention, two major areas of focus which have an immediate impact on the amount of Throughput being generated by the constraint are:

- Product Design/Redesign to minimize constraint resource time for each product being produced.
- Routing Changes for products which could be produced in a different way or on different resources.

In the product mix decision process in chapter five, it was discovered that the amount of Throughput generated for the constraint time used in making each product determined which product mix would be the most profitable. The lower the amount of constraint time per Throughput dollar created, the higher the amount of Throughput generated for the company. Those products which had the highest Throughput rating per unit of the constraint were given the first priority in absorbing constraint time. In the engineering process whenever products are being designed or redesigned careful consideration must be given to insuring that the amount of time for all products processed on the constraint is held to a minimum. As the ratio of Throughput per unit of the constraint goes up the amount of money coming into the company will also increase.

Process changes must also consider this issue. If a routing change can be made which decreases the constraint time used then the amount of money which can be made will increase.

In the activity based cost information presented in chapter five the following information was used to determine the most profitable product mix:

Routing Part A				Routing Part B		
Res	Op.	Time		Res	Op.	Time
123	10	10		123	10	10
124	20	30		124	20	15
125	30	20		125	30	20

Res	Time Avail.	Demand A	B	Total	Delta
123	7200	1000	2000	3000	+4200
124	5400	3000	3000	6000	- 600
125	7200	2000	4000	6000	+1200

	Mat.	Lab.	Ovr. Hd.	Std Cost	Sales Price	Prof. Mar.	Quan. Sold	Cash Gen.
A	80	60	60	200	300	100	80	17,600
B	80	60	180	320	310	-10	200	46,000
								63,600
								-60,000
								3 600

	A	B
Sales Price	300	310
Raw Material	80	80
Cash Generated	220/30 = $7.3	230/15 = $15.3

Resource 124 was identified as the limiting factor in that it needed 600 more hours to meet demand created by the market. Product A required 30 minutes of constraint time and generated $220 while product B used 15 minutes of constraint time and generated $230. The most profitable product was determined to be product B. For every minute of constraint time used $15.3 were created as compared to $7.3 for product A. So the determination was made to use as much constraint time making product B as possible. Any time left over would be used in making product A.

If the routing for product B were to change or if a modification was made which reduced the amount of time it took to make product B by one minute the result would be an increase in productive capability resulting in 200 minutes (one minute for every product B made and sold) being made available to make product A. The increase in Throughput would be immediate. An additional 6 As could be made which would result in an increase of $1320.

	Mat.	Lab.	Ovr. Hd.	Std Cost	Sales Price	Prof. Mar.	Quan. Sold	Cash Gen.
A	80	60	60	200	300	100	86	18,920*
B	80	60	180	320	310	-10	200	46,000
								64,920
								-60,000
								4,920

Almost anywhere time can be saved on the constraint will result in an increase in throughput. However, the process of determining where to focus the engineering effort begins with a Pareto analysis of demand. What product/operations use the most constraint time based on the current load? Part A uses 30 minutes of constraint time and 60 minutes total resource time while part B uses 15 minutes of constraint time and 45 minutes of total resource time. It would seem that the best place to look for improvements would be part A. However, the largest constraint load is actually created by part B with a total demand of 3,000 minutes compared to 2,400 minutes used by part A. In addition, each minute saved on part/operation B/20 will result in a total of 200 minutes being released to be used in making more As to meet market demand. Figure 9.16 is an illustration of a Pareto analysis of part/operations which cross the constraint.

While not all improvements will originate from first going through a Pareto analysis of part/operation demand, it is an excellent starting point in determining where to focus engineering improvements. Additional considerations include issues

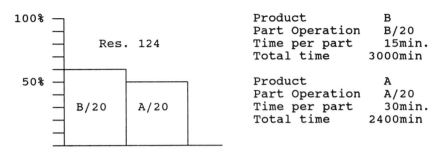

Figure 9.16   Exploiting the constraint.

of the reliability or capability of a given product or process. Obviously, if a product is difficult to make on the constraint it will take up more constraint time. The larger the time spent on the constraint, the smaller the opportunity is to create Throughput.

SUMMARY

Meeting the necessary conditions of the customer while designing products to increase productivity and protect the creation of Throughput is the objective of the product/process design system under TQM II. It is imperative that the designers become aware of their role in supporting the overall effort to increase profits.

10

Statistical Process Control (SPC)

This chapter is designed to provide a basic introduction to the process of statistical process control. It is used as a prerequisite to chapter eleven: Implementing SPC for Quality and Profit.

OBJECTIVES

- To introduce the concepts of variability and process capability.
- To create an understanding of the basic use of charts and the charting process.
- To learn how basic charts are constructed.
- To learn how to interpret charted data and devise solutions.

NORMAL VARIATION

Normal variations within a process create results which are predictable and, when plotted on a graph, the frequency of occurrences create what is normally referred to as a bell shaped curve. It is the predictability of the normal distribution, or curve, which can be used to determine whether a process is in control or is capable of creating a defect free part. As an example, the average person in the United States is reported to be five foot ten inches tall. With a little more information, it should be possible to predict how many people are of what height. When applied to manufacturing processes, statistics can be used to predict the size or distribution of sizes of different parts being produced from specific resources.

In a bell shaped curve the majority of occurrences should appear around the average or mean. Figure 10.1 illustrates.

Notice that the farther away from the center of the distribution, or mean, the fewer the number of occurrences.

$$\text{Mean} = \frac{\text{Sum Of Occurrences}}{\text{Total Number Of Occurrences}}$$

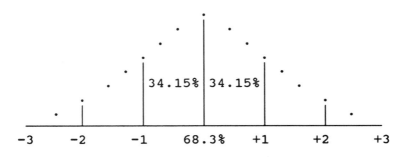

Figure 10.1   The bell shaped curve.

If the total range of the normal curve were to be divided into 6 equal segments called sigma, the majority, or 68.3%, of all measurements should fall within plus or minus one sigma.

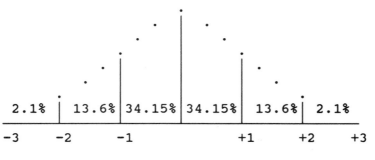

34.15% of the measurements taken should be between the mean, or average size, and minus one sigma. 34.15% of the measurements taken should equal the mean plus one sigma.

The remainder of the distribution should resemble figure 10.2 where 99.7% of all measurements would fall within plus or minus 3 sigma. If this does not occur then something abnormal is happening to the process.

Figure 10.2   Sigma in the normal curve.

Finding sigma for a process is not as easy as dividing the total range by six. What is being delt with is the probability that a number will fall within a certain measurement range. The smaller the sample size taken to arrive at sigma the smaller the probability of being correct.

A table, usually found in the back of statistics books, is used to designate multipliers for finding sigma based on the sample size taken. The formula for sigma reads as follows:

$$\text{Sigma} = \frac{\overline{R}}{D_2}$$

$\overline{R}$ is the average range of measurements taken. A sample size of five parts taken at different times would yield an average range. Range is equal to the highest value minus the lowest value within the same subgroup.

8:00	9:00	10:00	11:00	12:00
8	5	10	5	8
7	7	6	9	4
6	9	9	4	7
5	4	4	8	6
4	6	7	7	5

The range for the 8:00 sample is equal to 8 minus 4. The ranges for all samples are averaged to arrive at the average range which, in this case, is 4.8.

$$\text{Sigma} = \frac{\overline{R}}{D_2} = \frac{4.8}{2.326} = 2.06$$

Sample size	D_2
2	1.128
3	1.693
4	2.059
* 5	2.326
6	2.534
7	2.704

PROCESS CAPABILITY

Once an understanding of what a resource should be able to produce on a consistent basis is determined through statistical means, it must also be determined whether it can produce within engineering specifications. In determining whether a process is capable of producing parts consistently within engineering specification, the specification range must be divided by capability of the process. The specification range is determined by the engineering specification. Process capability is determined by multiplying sigma for the process times six. As an example, the specification for a given 1/4 inch bolt is .25 inches plus or minus .015. The range would be from plus .015 to a minus .015 or .030 inches. If sigma for the process were .00375, six sigma would be .00375 times six or .0225. The capability index (Cp) for the process would be:

$$Cp = \frac{\text{Specification Range}}{\text{Process Capability}} = \frac{.030}{.0225} = 1.33$$

Note: With a Cp of less than 1.33 the process is considered incapable of consistently producing defect free parts.

In this case, the mean of the process and the midpoint of the specification or target value were both .25 inches. In the following figure the process capability and the specification have been graphically represented.

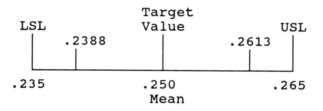

But what would be the impact if the mean of the process were to shift in either the plus or minus direction while the six sigma spread remained the same? It would mean that there would be an increased probability of defects appearing on the end of the specification toward which the shift were made.

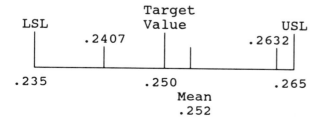

To insure that the capability index reflects this change it must be modified. The Cpk index is used. The process for finding the Cpk index is:

- Find min.
- Divide Z min by 3.

Z min is found by first finding Z upper and Z lower. Once this has been found the lowest of the two becomes Z min.

$$\text{Z upper} = \frac{|\text{Upper Specification Limit - Mean}|}{\text{Sigma}}$$

$$\text{Z lower} = \frac{|\text{Lower Specification Limit - Mean}|}{\text{Sigma}}$$

Notice that the numerator in the equation is an absolute number. In otherwords any negative numbers are converted to positive numbers.

$$\text{Cpk} = \frac{\text{Z min}}{3}$$

Z upper for the process described above is

$$\text{Z upper} = \frac{.265 - .252}{.00375} = 3.46$$

Z lower for the process described above is

$$\text{Z lower} = \frac{.235 - .252}{.00375} = 4.53$$

Z min is the lower of the two and is

$$\text{Z min} = 3.46$$

Cpk is

$$\text{Cpk} = \frac{3.46}{3} = 1.15$$

Since the mean of the process shifted to the right, the Cpk dropped from 1.33 to 1.15 and the process is no longer considered capable of consistently producing defect free parts.

QUANTIFYING THE EXPECTED LOSS

To determine the number of defective parts expected for the either side of the specification the figures for Z upper and Z lower are compared against a table for determining the area under the normal curve. See table A.1 in the Appendix. In the above case Z upper was 3.46. By finding 3.4 on the table under the Z and moving across to .00027 under the 0.06 and then moving the decimal over 2 places to the right the percentile figure is determined. For a Z upper of 3.46 a reject rate of .027% can be expected. There will also be a reject rate expected for Z lower and it can be found in the same manner. A Z lower of 4.53 will result in a .00029% reject rate. When added together the total reject rate expected is .02729%. Note: In Appendix A.1 the single numbers just to the right of the Z column indicate the number of zeros which should appear to the left of the entry. As an example when finding the expected loss for Z upper, 3.46, three zeros were added to the left of the 27009 and the last three digits were rounded up. For Z lower five zeros were added to the left of the entry.

It will be important to determine which side of the specification will determine a rework and which side will determine a scrap. Its global impact will be discussed in chapter eleven on Implementing SPC for Quality and Profit.

X-BAR AND R CHART CONSTRUCTION

The first step in the charting process is to construct the chart. Located at the top of most charts is the administrative area which may include the part name and number, the operation, the name of the operator, specifications, the gauge to be used, etc. See figure 10.3

Most of this is pretty much self explanatory. Specification limits refers to the engineering specification. The zero base is a number used in the coding process. It is not always desirable to maintain exact copies of measurements. To shorten the amount of work necessary as well as to simplify the process, coding is used. Coding involves several different methods for reducing the amount of data used but is basically the subtraction of a number from actual data to create a smaller

Part Number	Nomenclature			
12345	Armature Flying Grammis			

Operator	Machine/Op.	UOM	Zero Base	Engineering Spec.
John	LATHE 123	.001	.500	.500 - .515

Figure 10.3 The X-Bar and R chart.

number. When added back, the original number is recreated. Zero base numbers for coding include:

- Common Number—A number which is common to all numbers in the base data collected.
- The Target Value—The target value is the midpoint of the engineering specification.
- The Smallest Measurement—The smallest measurement within the base data collected.
- Largest Measurement—The largest measurement within the base data collected.
- Nice Round Number—Any number which can be easily subtracted from the data collected.
- The upper or lower specification limit.

As an example, the numbers .510, .509, .508, and .504 represent actual measurements. To reduce these numbers to smaller sizes establish the zero base and subtract. If the zero base were set at .500 then the coded numbers would equal 10, 9, 8, and 4. If it were set at the lowest measurement the coded numbers would be 6, 5, 4, and 0. The lowest measurement is .504. When added to 6 the number would be .510.

Just under the administrative area is the section used to record measurements and to compute range and average figures. The bottom half is used to plot measurements graphically and to set certain control mechanisms. Once the zero base has been established and the sampling plan has been set data collection can begin. The initial objective is to collect enough information to understand what the average mean and average range for a particular operation are and to create the centerline for the average and range sections in the bottom half of the chart. At least 20 measurements are necessary to do this. The sampling plan and data used in the capability section is still applicable.

8:00	9:00	10:00	11:00	12:00
8	5	10	5	8
7	7	6	9	4
6	9	9	4	7
5	4	4	8	6
4	6	7	7	5

The plan was to inspect five consecutive parts from the object process every hour. At the end of five hours twenty-five parts had been inspected. The measurements are entered on the chart under the applicable time in the sample measurements section. See figure 10.4.

Time	8:00	9:00	10:00	11:00	12:00
S M	8	5	10	5	8
a e	7	7	6	9	4
m a					
p s	6	9	9	4	7
l u					
e r	5	4	4	8	6
e					
s	4	6	7	7	5

Figure 10.4 The measurement samples.

Directly under the sample measurements section is a section for entering the sum, the average and the range for the measurements taken. The sum is determined by adding the measurements. Once added, by dividing the sum by subgroup sample size, the mean is determined. The range is determined by subtracting the high measurement from the low within subgroup samples. Figure 10.5 is the results of the measurements from figure 10.4.

The notes section is used to enter any process changes and may give clues for determining the causes of any changes in the measurements which indicate an out of control situation.

To begin filling the average and range plotting sections the grand average and average range must be determined first. The grand average is determined by finding the sum of all the averages from left to right and then dividing by the number of averages used. The average range is determined by finding the sum of all ranges and dividing by the number of ranges used. Using the numbers from figure 10.5 the following is the computation for grand average and average range.

Sum	30	31	36	33	30
Average, X	6.0	6.2	7.2	6.6	6.0
Range, R	4	5	6	5	4
Notes					

Figure 10.5 Establishing the sum, average and range.

Grand Average $(\overline{\overline{X}})$ = 6.0 + 6.2 + 7.2 + 6.6 + 6.0 = 32/5 = 6.4

Average Range $(\overline{R})$ = 4 + 5 + 6 + 5 + 4 = 24/5 = 4.8

The grand average $(\overline{\overline{X}})$ and the average range $(\overline{R})$ are used to determine the average and range center lines for the chart in the plotting section. Once determined, the center lines can be set.

Sum	30	31	36	33	30
Average, X	6.0	6.2	7.2	6.6	6.0
Range, R	4	5	6	5	4
Notes					

```
A
v
e       _
r  X    6.4
a
g
e
```

```
R
a
n  R    4.8
g
e
```

Once the center lines have been created, control and warning limits are set so that out of control conditions can be easily detected and causes interpreted. Control limits are set at plus or minus 3 sigma from the grand average or from the average range. Warning limits are set at plus or minus 2 sigma. To set control and warning limits the following formulas are used:

Average (X)

Upper Control Limit $(UCL_{\overline{X}})$ = $\overline{\overline{X}} + A_2\overline{R}$ = 6.4 + (.577 × 4.8) = 9.17

Lower Control Limit $(LCL_{\overline{X}})$ = $\overline{\overline{X}} - A_2\overline{R}$ = 6.4 - (.577 × 4.8) = 3.63

$$\text{Upper Warning Limit (UWL}_{\overline{X}}) = \overline{\overline{X}} + 2 \left(\frac{A_2 \overline{R}}{3}\right) = 6.4 + 2 \left(\frac{.577 \times 4.8}{3}\right) = 8.25$$

$$\text{Lower Warning Limit (LWL}_{\overline{X}}) = \overline{\overline{X}} - 2 \left(\frac{A_2 \overline{R}}{3}\right) = 6.4 - 2 \left(\frac{.577 \times 4.8}{3}\right) = 4.55$$

Range (R)

$$\text{Upper Control Limit (UCL}_R) = D_4 \overline{R} = 2.115 \times 4.8 = 10.15$$

$$\text{Upper Warning Limit (UWL}_R) = 2 \left(\frac{D_4 \overline{R} - \overline{R}}{3}\right) + \overline{R} = 2 \left(\frac{2.115 \times 4.8 - 4.8}{3}\right) + 4.8$$

$$= 8.37$$

Figure 10.6 represents the table of factors for computing control and warning limits.

Once the upper and lower control and warning limits have been determined the charts should be updated with a heavy dotted line for each so that it can be easily determined if a problem exists.

Subgroup Size	A_2	D_4
2	1.880	3.267
3	1.023	2.575
4	.729	2.282
* 5	.577	2.115
6	.483	2.004
7	.419	1.924

Figure 10.6 Table of factors..

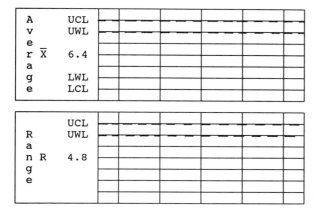

PLOTTING

After the chart has been prepared the plotting can begin. The numbers to be plotted include the average and range for each subgroup. For each subgroup a separate plot is made using as a reference the centerline established earlier and the time in which the subgroup sample was taken. See figure 10.7.

SPC CHART INTERPRETATION

The objective of chart interpretation is to determine whether a process is under control and if not to determine what might be causing out of control conditions. In both the average and range charts below, under normal variation, 68.3% of all measurements should fall within plus or minus 1 sigma of the centerline measurement, 95.5% within 2 sigma and 99.7% within 3 Sigma. If this does not happen something is wrong with the process. It has an abnormal variation.

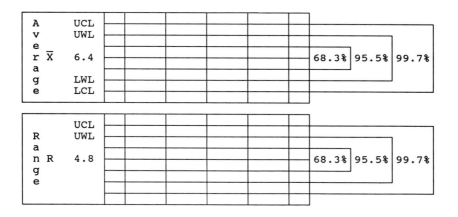

Time	8:00	9:00	10:00	11:00	12:00
S M	8	5	10	5	8
a e	7	7	6	9	4
m a					
p s	6	9	9	4	7
l u					
e r	5	4	4	8	6
e					
s	4	6	7	7	5

	8:00	9:00	10:00	11:00	12:00
Sum	30	31	36	33	30
Average, X	6.0	6.2	7.2	6.6	6.0
Range, R	4	5	6	5	4
Notes					

```
A       UCL
v       UWL
e
r  X̄   6.4
a
g       LWL
e       LCL
```

```
        UCL
R       UWL
a
n  R   4.8
g
e
```

Figure 10.7 Plotting.

There are different rules for abnormal patterns which indicate that certain conditions may exist in the process. They are:

Freaks—Any one point outside 3 sigma on either side of the centerline.

- Major causes are usually human error such as arithmetic, plotting or measurement. Also caused by material problems.

Freak Patterns—Two out of three measurements outside two sigma on either side of the centerline.

- Four out of five measurements outside one sigma on either side of the centerline.
- Usually caused by material or measurement problems.

Shifts—Seven measurements in a row on one side of the centerline.

- Usually caused by a change in material, machine speed or setup.

Trends—Six measurements in a row each above the last measurement or Six measurements in a row each below the last measurement.

- Caused by a gradual change such as tool wear.

```
A      UCL
v      UWL
e
r  X̄   6.4
a
g      LWL
e      LCL
```

Cyclical Patterns—Patterns which repeat themselves.

- Usually caused by human factors such as shift changes. May also be caused by defective equipment.

```
A      UCL
v      UWL
e
r  X̄   6.4
a
g      LWL
e      LCL
```

Jumps—A movement of 4 sigma or more between two consecutive measurements.

- A jump usually indicates that something has broken.

```
A      UCL
v      UWL
e
r  X̄   6.4
a
g      LWL
e      LCL
```

Stable Mixtures—Five points in a row outside one sigma on both sides of the centerline with no points within one sigma.

- Usually indicates the mixture of two different processes. One major cause is material related. Can also be caused by different operators or measuring equipment.

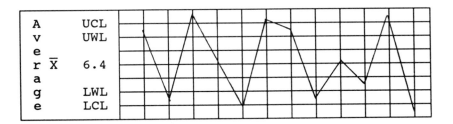

Clustering—Measurements which occur in clusters all over the chart.

- Indicative of mixing materials from different vendors or processes. Causes can be man, material, machine, method, or tooling

Erratic Patterns—With ten measurements plotted 40% are outside two sigma or 30% outside three sigma.

- Primary causes include operator error, over adjustment or inconsistent measurement

Stratification—Fourteen points in a row inside one sigma.

- Caused by not measuring to a fine enough tolerance or by operators fudging the figures.

Once a pattern has been identified a cause is then speculated and a solution implemented which will bring the pattern back into normal distribution. Tools for solving problems in out of control conditions include brainstorming to assimilate speculative causes and possible solutions. Fishbone analysis for organizing the process and design of experiments which deals with the impact of large numbers of variables in finding alternatives.

ADDITIONAL CHARTS

The X-Bar and R charts are usually used to track variable type data, that is data which is measured. In addition to variables type charts there are also charts which record attribute data, or data which are simple good/bad decisions. The key issue here is the number or percent of defectives or defects which may occur. These additional charts include the p chart and its derivatives for controlling parts defective, and the c and u charts for controlling specific defects or the quality characteristics within the part.

Note: The amount of time allowed for control charts was to give the reader a better understanding of SPC prior to the discussion of implementation. It has been simplified so that a better understanding of chapter eleven could be established. For a complete discussion of SPC under the traditional approach, see Statistical Process Control by Leonard A. Doty, Industrial Press, (1991).

• • •

How to implement SPC and where to focus has undergone tremendous change.

• • •

11

Implementing SPC For Quality And Profit

This chapter is dedicated to understanding how to properly implement SPC to support the necessary condition of good quality and the process of continuous profit improvement.

OBJECTIVES

- To establish the relationship between the way in which resources interface and SPC.
- To understand those areas within the production process which have the greatest impact on the SPC implementation.
- To understand how the SPC program is used in the exploitation and subordination phases.
- To create the relationship between the SPC program and customer demand.
- To establish the relationship between the SPC implementation and its impact on the decision process.
- To establish the implementation procedure and to address those actions which will block it.

Under TQM II SPC is used to continuously support the exploitation and subordination phases within the five step process so that Throughput can be enhanced or protected and to support the QFD program in meeting customer requirements. To do this the implementor must know where to focus, how to implement and how to prevent being blocked.

FOCUSING THE SPC EFFORT

As expressed in earlier chapters, the global impact of an improvement cannot be established based on a localized measurement such as reject rates. To understand

175

what is important in implementing SPC a method must be used to determine the relationships between resources so that global issues can be addressed. To do this the product flow diagram is used. Figure 11.1 illustrates.

As discussed in Chapter three, the product flow diagram is a detailed description of the flow of product from the gating operation to the sales order. Included in the basic diagram is:

- The bill of material, designating the part number and determining product levels.
- The routing, designating the sequence of operations.
- Resource information, designating where an operation is to be performed.

As in the previous example resource load information has been added giving an indication as to the severity of a particular problem from a global perspective. Those resources which can least afford a problem are those which are expected to accomplish the most. However, there are more subtle issues to be addressed.

- The string of resources leading from the constraint to the sales order.
- Those resources whose characteristics are prerequisites for the constraint.
- Those resources whose characteristics are prerequisites for QFD.
- Those resources which create holes in the Buffer due to rework or scrap.

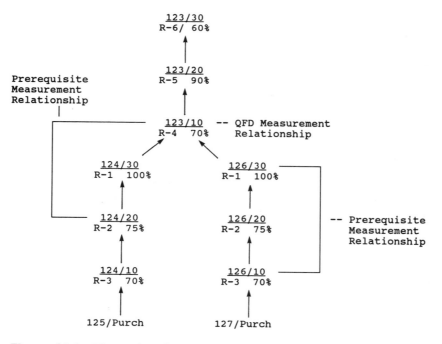

Figure 11.1 The product flow diagram.

In figure 11.1, resource R-1 is considered the constraint since it is loaded to 100%. R-4, R-5 and R-6 represent the string of resources leading from the constraint to the sales order. In processing orders from resource R-1 through R-6 great care must be used to insure that no scrap occurs. Products being processed on the constraint or which have already been through it are considered more valuable than those which have not. Constraint time governs the amount of Throughput which can be generated. Its limited availability means that no additional parts can be made without sacrificing Throughput. Resource R-5 also has a limitation in capacity. Its being loaded to 90% means the chances are very good that the orders going through this resource will be late. It can ill afford rework as well. Resources R-4 and R-6 have additional capacity to handle rework.

While not originally presented in the product flow diagram an examination of product specifications finds that the prerequisites for creating acceptable measurements at part/operation 126/30, performed on resource R-1, is the measurements attained at part/operation 126/10, performed on R-3. An over or undersized measurement could result in scrap or rework at 126/30, on resource R-1, the constraint.

Also not considered is the impact of QFD. An examination of the QFD matrix diagram shows a very high relationship between the measurements attained at part/operation 123/10, performed on resource R-4, and customer requirements. There has also been found a measurement relationship between 123/10, performed on R-4, and 124/20, performed on R-2.

What does all this mean to the implementation of SPC? The first implication is the sequencing of the implementation. Those resources having problems and impact Throughput the most are the ones which should be implemented first. If a scrap or rework problem were impacting the constraint, or would cause the necessary conditions required by 123/10 on R-4 to be missed, obviously a study of the capability and an implementation of statistical control of resource R-1 and R-4 would be highly recommended. The second implication is in the improvement process. Those resources which restrict Throughput should be improved first.

There are also implications for those resources which are not capable but must perform and how to minimize the damage to Throughput. After examining the product flow diagram it was discovered that certain resources, because of capacity, location and customer requirements were required to fulfill certain quality related responsibilities which included:

- The prevention of scrap.
- The prevention of any type of loss.
- The support of QFD.
- The support of other resources.

It was learned that R-1 and R-5 were critical because of the load placed on them. Any loss from these two resources, whether rework or scrap, will result in either a permanent loss of throughput or a delayed order. To minimize any loss the Cpk index should be 1.33 or better at these part/operation/resources and all attempts made to keep them in control. Resources R-4 and R-6, while they can take a certain amount of rework, cannot afford scrap and all attempts should be made to prevent it. Work improvement team efforts should include as a priority any loss on R-1 and R-5 and any scrap on R-4 and R-6.

ADAPTING TO CAPABILITY

In conditions where the Cpk is less than 1.33, by moving the mean for the operation toward the rework side of the specification scrap could be minimized. Since additional capacity is available to complete rework and still finish the order on time, Throughput would not be threatened. However, there may be design implications to this issue as well as the impact to other resource capability. Products are designed to fit together around the nominal of the specification. If the mean of the process distribution is to be moved, the means of other resources as well as design specifications will need examining.

In certain cases, the constraint will have a low Cpk index and either scrap or rework is unavoidable. The best alternative might be to move the constraint by elevating the constraint resource using whatever means are available. This is not always possible. The issue now becomes how to minimize the amount of damage incurred. To be able to totally understand the result, the cumulative impact of scrap or rework must be known across the entire schedule horizon. The key issues being:

- The cumulative value of the time taken from the constraint in Throughput terms by either rework or scrap.
- The cumulative value of the raw material loss projection due to scrap.
- The increase in Inventory or Operating Expense, if any, due to an increase in load requirements on non, or near, constraint resources existing prior to the constraint and caused by recreating the replacement parts.

To answer this question means than a valid schedule must be produced for both alternatives and the impact determined from the results.

THE IMPACT ON PRODUCT MIX

There are other considerations. A decision of how to maximize profitability given the current limitations must still be made. The additional time needed to process the part on the constraint due to rework or scrap will add to the total time used to process the part. Not only has there been an impact on the utilization of constraint time, but, there will also be an impact on the product mix decision as well (see Chapter five). The amount of constraint time absorbed by the product is a key issue. See figure 11.2. The formula for the decision is:

$$\frac{\text{Throughput}}{\text{Total Constraint Time Per Unit}}$$

The amount of Throughput generated by part A and B each time they are sold is $100. For product A the amount of constraint time absorbed is 40 minutes and the amount for product B is 30 minutes making product B more profitable at $3.33 per constraint minute. However, when rework is considered product A becomes more profitable. B's total constraint absorption increases from 30 minutes to 60 minutes. And the Throughput per unit of the constraint declines to $1.66.

What has not been considered in this problem is the rate of rework for the current schedule. On average, the amount of rework may be 10% or three min-

	Product	(Rework) Product
	A	B
Throughput Generated	$100	$100
Original CCR Time per unit	40 min.	30 min.
Throughput per unit of the Constraint	$2.50	$3.33
Additional CCR Time per unit Due to Rework		30 min
Total CCR Time per unit	40 min	60 min
Throughput per unit of the Constraint	$2.50	$1.66

Figure 11.2 The impact on product mix. CCR = capacity-constrained resource.

utes additional CCR time for all product Bs in the horizon. Instead of using the full 30 minute rework time, the reduced value of 3 minutes or 10% of 30 minutes is used. Product B then becomes the most profitable.

	A	B
Total CCR Time per unit	40 min	33 min
Throughput per unit of the Constraint	$2.50	$3.03

With scrap the situation is similar except that the loss due to having to replace the raw material must be included in the equation as well. The amount of Throughput generated per unit must be reduced by the raw material cost. Throughput for B (Scrap) is computed as Throughput minus raw material. Throughput has been reduced from $100 to $75.

	(Scrap) Product B	(Rework) Product B
Throughput Generated	$ 75	$100
Total CCR Time per unit	30 min.	45 min.
Throughput per unit of Constraint Time	$2.50	$2.22

In this case it would be more profitable to scrap the product than rework since the Throughput per unit of the constraint is higher.

In considering process/product design issues, in this case, it would be more profitable to set the mean of the distribution of measurements for the constraint resource to the scrap side of the specification or move the nominal of the specification to minimize rework. In this way the constraint would be making $2.50 per minute instead of $2.22. However, this decision must be made from a global perspective and should include the impact on other resources as well as the final product. If the mean of a process is changed it may affect what becomes acceptable product at other processes. Products are designed so that the nominal of each specification matches.

Those resources which are prerequisites to the constraint and have a Cpk of less than 1.33 should be judged, like all decisions, based on their impact on Throughput, Inventory and Operating Expense. Whether there is a positive or negative relationship between SPC charts, the mean of the prerequisite resource should be moved to minimize the impact on the constraints ability to create Throughput and the generation of Inventory and Operating Expense. Scrap on non-constraint resources occurring before the constraint will lose the value of raw material. Rework on those same resources has no value unless protective capacity is used.

Based on the product flow diagram, increasing capacity at resource R-1 would probably move the CCR to resource R-5, a resource which is loaded to 90%. If R-1 had a Cpk of 1.00 and R-5 had a Cpk of 1.33, this might be the right approach to take. However, there are other considerations. Moving the CCR to R-5 would also shorten the distance from the constraint to the sales order. Scrap on resources R-4 and R-1 would then play a much smaller role.

Once those resources which are critical to the generation of Throughput have been brought under control the impact to other resources can be addressed. Those resources which create holes in the buffer caused by out of control conditions should be addressed as well. The buffer management process should indicate those resources which were causing consistent delays in reaching the buffer origin.

PRODUCTS DESIGNED AROUND THE MIDDLE OF THE SPECIFICATION

There is another consideration which has not been addressed—the cumulative impact of resources whose means are not grouped around the nominal value of the specification. Two parts, designed to be fitted together whose measurements are at the wrong ends of the specification may not fit at all. A prime example of this occurring is with nuts and bolts. A bolt may have an outside dimension of 1/4 inch plus or minus .015 inches. A nut may have an internal dimension of 1/4 plus or minus .015 inches. The nominal value would be 1/4 inch. However, If the mean of the process which produced the bolt was set at 1/4 inch minus .015 it would produce bolts which were undersized. If the mean of the process which produced the nut were set at 1/4 inch minus .015 it would be producing nuts which were undersized as well. The result is mismatched parts. It may be easier to insure that the means of processes are matched to the target value of the specification than it is to wait until there is an impact on Throughput.

THE IMPLEMENTATION SEQUENCE

As in the implementation of any complex process a logical sequence of events should be used to assure a smooth transition. The following is a suggestion for the implementation of SPC.

- Develop the product flow diagram.
- Establish buffer management.
- Identify critical operations.
- List in order of criticality based on their impact to Throughput.
- Choose the quality characteristics to be charted.
- Implement the pilot project.
- Schedule the remaining charts to be implemented.
- Organize a committee for each chart.
- Collect data, plot charts and develop Cpk indexes.
- Analyze charts as data becomes available.
- Correct assignable causes based on the impact to Throughput.

In choosing the quality characteristic it is very important to choose those characteristics which, if kept in control, will maximize Throughput. Candidates include:

- Those characteristics which represent a large portion of Throughput generated by the constraint.
- Those characteristics required by QFD and are critical to the primary function of the product.
- Those characteristics which serve as prerequisites to the constraint.
- Those characteristics which may negatively effect work completed on the constraint.
- Those characteristics whose rejects are causing holes in the buffer.

In implementing a pilot project it is wise to begin with a resource which is having a major impact on Throughput due to rework or scrap. Any success here will create the support needed to extend the process to other resources. If unaware of a specific resource which is having this type of problem, begin with the constraint. Once the resource is selected begin the charting process and develop the Cpk index. The remaining charts should be implemented based on their impact to Throughput, Inventory and Operating Expense.

In organizing a committee for each chart, the objective is to insure that when an improvement must be found the right people are there to find it. This committee may include a representative from engineering, the operator, the supervisor of the area and quality assurance. Each committee should have people who understand general problem solving techniques such as brainstorming, fishbone analysis, design of experiments, etc.

Buffer management can begin at any time during the implementation of SPC. However, it is preferred that it begin as one of the first steps in the process so that the benefits of using the aggregated impact of problems on the buffer origin can be gained.

OVERCOMING BLOCKING ACTIONS

One of the biggest problems seen in making SPC successful is a lack of understanding of what it is and where it should be used. What SPC is can easily be solved through education. But, where it should be used is a different issue. Many problems must be overcome much the same as an implementation of TQM II. The basic blockers to a successful implementation include:

- Conflicting goals and measurements.
- Poor decision systems and support mechanisms.
- Lack of understanding of how to meet the necessary conditions.
- A lack of understanding of how resources interface and the resulting impact on the system.
- The cost mentality.
- Failure to understand how to motivate people.

These are the same basic reasons for preventing a successful implementation of SPC. In implementing SPC different people, because of their position, may block in different ways; managers and supervisors by issuing invalid priorities or withholding resources; workers by charting incorrectly, refusing to chart or by not reacting correctly to problems encountered. Most people can understand, when presented logically, how to implement, the importance, where to chart, etc. But, in getting managers, supervisors and workers to implement successfully motivation may be the biggest issue. You must win their hearts and minds well enough to overcome their current tendencies. It seems that the hearts and minds of company presidents are being won over by customers who are making SPC a necessary condition by requiring SPC charts before placing orders. However, the difference between a successful implementation of SPC and an unsuccessful one will depend on the impact to profitability not just from a customer perspective but from all aspects. Fulfilling the necessary condition will only insure that customer's are happy. It doesn't insure that profitability will continually rise.

The biggest problem in motivation is fear and "not invented here". These issues must be overcome. One method being used with growing success is the Socratic Method. It is involved in supporting the process of having people invent their own solutions. In theory the inventor is the only person not effected by fear or "not invented here". In order to implement, the subject is place in a situation, given a set of guidelines and then asked to find a solution. This can be done using simulators, by asking just the right question or by using the policy analysis process described in chapter four. It is very important not to give the answers. Once given, the student is immediately blocked from discovering them himself or realizing the truth.

12

Design of Experiments (DOE)

This chapter will use the Taguchi Method as an introduction to the DOE process and will explore how the DOE process should be used in support of the five step improvement process.

OBJECTIVES

- To create a basic understanding of the experimental design concept.
- To design a two level and multi-level experiment.
- To conduct an analysis of variance through the use of the ANOVA table.
- To gain insight into how to use the DOE methods to support the exploitation and subordination processes.
- To explore the validity of the Taguchi loss function as a focusing mechanism.

DESIGN OF EXPERIMENTS (DOE) DEFINED

The objective of the designed experiment is to understand the impact of specific changes to the inputs of a process, and then to maximize, minimize, or nominalize the outcome by manipulating the input. It is usually used when it is unclear what impact a specific set of inputs may have, either individually or collectively, on a process. By constructing the experiment in a specific way and recording the resulting impact, or observation, it is possible to understand what impact each variable within the process has and the degree of result.

Multiple runs or trials are made while manipulating each input or group of inputs and the resulting observations are recorded. An analysis of the inputs as well as the result will determine the level of input needed to arrive at the optimum result.

<u>Inputs</u>   <u>Output</u>

Man
_____

Material
_____

Machine
_____   ┌─────────────────┐
                                         │   │
Method   │   Process   │   Result
_____   │   │
                                         └─────────────────┘
Tool
_____

Environment
_____

DESIGNING THE EXPERIMENT

The first step in conducting the designed experiment is to determine the quality characteristic to be examined and the desired effect. This is probably the most important step and should be examined carefully. Brainstorming sessions are usually used to gain insight into what the goal of the experiment should be and to understand what factors (man, method, machine, material, tools and the environment) as well as levels within factors, might impact the goal. The Fishbone Chart is usually used to gather and organize information in the brainstorming sessions of about 10–12 people with various technical backgrounds so that a thorough cause and effect investigation can be performed.

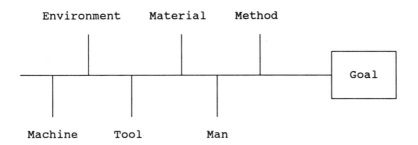

A level is a certain aspect of the factors chosen for the experiment. As an example, specific temperatures would be levels within the methods factor while drill bit types would be levels within the tools factor.

Factors	Tool	Method	Material	Machine
Levels	Carbide	100 Degrees C	Stainless	Lathe 1
	Titanium	150 Degrees C	Tungsten	Lathe 2

Once a set of factor/levels has been selected specific treatments are determined. A treatment is a specific set of factor/levels combined into one test. Each test of the same treatment is called a trial. Each trial will have an outcome or observation.

TWO LEVEL EXPERIMENTS (THE TAGUCHI METHOD)

The two level experiment is so named because it involves an experiment with a limited the number of levels (two within each factor). Once the goal for the experiment as well as the factors and levels to be tested have been selected, specific combinations of levels are arranged so that each treatment will be different and then the test trials are run. The results are recorded on the orthogonal array. An orthogonal array is a matrix used to plan and control the experiment. The orthogonal array in figure 12.1 presents four different treatments or mixtures of factor levels and two levels for each of three factors. Each treatment is read from left to right. Two trials or runs were held for each treatment and the results recorded under observations.

Notice that for each treatment the mixture of levels is never the same. In treatment 1, all level 1 factors are used. In treatment 2, level 1 for factor 1 is mixed with level 2 for factors 2 and 3. In this way each level will be used with every other level. Notice also that each level is used twice within each factor. Level 1 for factor 1 is used in treatments 1 and 2. Level 2 for factor 1 is used in treatments 3 and 4 and so on. By using this limited data and determining the impact each level will have on the observations it is possible to arrive at the optimum mix of levels which will produce the desired result.

For the experiment, the impact of process speed, temperature and wave height factors has been chosen for their impact on bridging as a result of problems encountered at the wave solder machine for a printed circuit board manufacturer. The objective is to minimize bridging resulting from the wave solder by finding just

Treatments	Factor 1	Factor 2	Factor 3	Observations	
1	Level 1	Level 1	Level 1	Trial 1	Trial 2
2	Level 1	Level 2	Level 2	Trial 1	Trial 2
3	Level 2	Level 1	Level 2	Trial 1	Trial 2
4	Level 2	Level 2	Level 1	Trial 1	Trial 2

Figure 12.1 The Orthogonal Array.

the right combination of speed temperature and wave solder height. Specific levels for elements were chosen as follows:

	Low	High
Temperature	475 Degrees F	510 Degrees F
Wave Height	.25 inches	.30 Inches
Process Speed	4 feet per minute	5 feet per minute

Under the Taguchi method, the low measurements are placed in the level one positions while the high are placed in the level two positions within the orthogonal array. After the trials have been run for each treatment the observations are also added.

For the experiment, observations are recorded as the total number of bridges per subgroup sample of 5 boards. The trial is run for a specific group of five boards and then bridging measured. The next trial is run with the next group of five boards. This continues until all trials and treatments have been completed and observations recorded.

Treatments	Temp.	Height	Speed	Observations	
1	475 F	.25 in	4 fpm	14	10
2	475 F	.30 in	5 fpm	30	21
3	510 F	.25 in	5 fpm	20	10
4	510 F	.30 in	4 fpm	37	20

Once the array has been completed the actual measurements for each level and the names for each factor are abbreviated so that the array resembles the following.

Treatments	T	H	S	Observations	
1	1	1	1	14	10
2	1	2	2	30	21
3	2	1	2	20	10
4	2	2	1	37	20

Level 1 measurements are replaced by a 1. Level 2 measurements are replaced by a 2 and each factor is abbreviate by using, in this case, the first letter of the descriptive title. Now focus can be concentrated on analyzing the observations without allot of detail.

The first step is to determine how much variation has occurred between all treatments. The total variation which has occurred is determined by adding the square of each observation together. Commonly referred to as the sum of squares.

$$\sum_i x^2 = 14^2 + 10^2 + 30^2 + 21^2 + 20^2 + 10^2 + 37^2 + 20^2$$

$$= 3906$$

The next step is to distribute this variation among a number of different types of variation which can occur including:

- The variation caused by the item being tested, in this case the wave solder machine—Grand Mean Effect.
- The variation caused by the individual factors within the experiment—Effect of Factors.
- The variation caused by the number of trials which are performed—Repetitional Error Effect.

EFFECT OF THE GRAND MEAN

The grand mean is determined by first summing the observations, squaring them and then dividing by the number of observations

$$\frac{\left[\sum_i x\right]^2}{n} = \frac{\left[14 + 10 + 30 + 21 + 20 + 10 + 37 + 20\right]^2}{8}$$

$$= \frac{162^2}{8} = \frac{26244}{8} = 3280.5$$

EFFECT OF THE FACTORS

The effect of the factors is determined by adding the level one observations together for each trial by factor, adding the level two observations together for each trial by factor and then subtracting the level two factor from the level one and squaring the result for each factor. The result is then divided by the total number of observations. The formula for the effect of temperature is written as follows:

$$S_T = \frac{\left[S_1 - S_2 \right]^2}{n}$$

In figure 12.2 the level one observations have been identified for temperature. Each observation for level one is added together

$$14 + 10 + 30 + 21 = 75$$

In figure 12.3 the level two observations have been identified for temperature. Each observation for level two is added together.

$$20 + 10 + 37 + 20 = 87$$

Treatments	T	H	S	Observations	
1	1	1	1	14	10
2	1	2	2	30	21
3	2	1	2	20	10
4	2	2	1	37	20

Figure 12.2   Level one observations for temperature.

Treatments	T	H	S	Observations	
1	1	1	1	14	10
2	1	2	2	30	21
3	2	1	2	20	10
4	2	2	1	37	20

Figure 12.3   Level two observations for temperature.

The Effect of temperature is

$$S_T = \frac{\left[75 - 87\right]^2}{8} = \frac{144}{8} = 18$$

In figure 12.4 the level one observations have been identified for wave height. In figure 12.5 the level two observations have been identified for wave height. The effect of wave height is

$$S_H = \frac{\left[51 - 108\right]^2}{8} = \frac{3294}{8} = 406.13$$

Treatments	T	H	S	Observations	
1	1	1	1	14	10
2	1	2	2	30	21
3	2	1	2	20	10
4	2	2	1	37	20

Figure 12.4 Level one observations for wave height.

Treatments	T	H	S	Observations	
1	1	1	1	14	10
2	1	2	2	30	21
3	2	1	2	20	10
4	2	2	1	37	20

Figure 12.5 Level two observations for wave height.

The effect of speed is

$$S_s = \frac{\left[84 - 81\right]^2}{8} = \frac{9}{8} = \mathbf{1.13}$$

REPETITIONAL ERROR EFFECT

The repetitional error effect can be determined by subtracting all other effects from the total variation. The formula for finding the repetitional error effect for the experiment is

$$S_{e2} = S_T - S_m - \left[S_T + S_W + S_s\right]$$

The repetitional error effect is

$$S_{e2} = 3906 - 3280.5 - \left[18 + 406.13 + 1.13\right] = \mathbf{200.24}$$

DETERMINING SIGNIFICANT FACTORS

The next step in the process is to determine which factors are significant and which are not. While at this point it is obvious that wave height is far more significant than speed and temperature there are other things to consider. To understand the significants of each measurement the minimum variance required for a measurement to be considered significant must be determined. This is calculated by dividing the repetitional error effect by the degrees of freedom and then multiplying the result times the F-value. The degrees of freedom is determined by adding one to the total number of factors in the experiment and subtracting the result from the total number of trials.

```
Degrees Of Freedom  =  Total Number Of Trials - Total Number
                       Of Factors  +  One

Degrees Of Freedom  =  8 - (3 + 1)  =  4
```

In this case there are three factors plus one is four, there are eight trials. The degrees of freedom are eight minus four equals four. The F-factor is taken from the F distribution table in Appendix A.2. The degrees of freedom is used to find the F-value. In this case the F-value is row four column one on the F distribution chart and equals 7.71.

```
Minimum Significant       Repetitional error effect
Variance          =      ─────────────────────────  x F-Value
                             Degrees Of Freedom


                         200.24
                  =      ─────── x  7.71  =  385.96
                            4

   Variance For Wave Height  =   406.13

   Minimum Significant       =   385.96
   Variance
```

Since the variance for wave height is greater than the minimum significant variance, wave height is a critical issue. Speed and temperature were considered non-significant. Had a significant measurement not been found the obviously insignificant factors could be dropped and the minimum significant variance recalculated. Since speed and temperature were not considered significant the degrees of freedom would need to be recalculated. In this case there would only be one factor in the formula

```
Degrees Of Freedom  =   Total Number Of Trials - (Total Number
                            Of Factors  +  One)

Degrees Of Freedom  =   8 - (1 + 1)  =  6
```

The F-value in this case would change. See Appendix A.2. Since the degrees of freedom have changed to 6 the F-value for a two level experiment and one factor will be 5.99.

```
Minimum Significant       Repetitional error effect
Variance          =      ─────────────────────────  x F-Value
                             Degrees Of Freedom


                         200.24
                  =      ─────── x  5.99  =  199.88
                            6
```

DETERMINING OPTIMUM RESULTS

By determining which levels within the wave height factor create the best average results the optimum setting for wave height can be determined.

Treatments	T	H	S	Observations	
1	1	1	1	14	10
2	1	2	2	30	21
3	2	1	2	20	10
4	2	2	1	37	20

$$\text{Average result (Level One)} = \frac{(14 + 10 + 20 + 10)}{4} = 13.5$$

The average results using the first level is 13.5.

Treatments	T	H	S	Observations	
1	1	1	1	14	10
2	1	2	2	30	21
3	2	1	2	20	10
4	2	2	1	37	20

$$\text{Average result (Level Two)} = \frac{(30 + 21 + 37 + 20)}{4} = 27$$

The average for the second level is 27. Since the objective is to minimize the amount of bridging on printed circuit boards the best optimum wave height for this experiment is level one or .25 inches while the settings for speed and temperature are insignificant.

CONDUCTING LARGER EXPERIMENTS

Experiments will often be larger than two levels with three factors and two trials as presented in the two level experiment. To conduct larger experiments there are a few basic changes. However the concept is roughly the same. The key issue is to insure that the experiment is constructed around the proper factors and levels before proceeding. In the wave solder experiment conducted earlier the shape of the wave has become an issue, the number of trials has increased from two to three, the number of factors has increased and the number of observations have also changed.

	Low	Med.	High
Temperature	475 F	490 F	510 F
Wave Height	.25 in.	.27 in.	.30 in.
Process Speed	4 fpm	4.5 fpm	5 fpm
Wave Shape	1	2	3

T	H	S	W	Observations			
1	1	1	1	15	27	22	17
1	2	2	2	30	21	36	27
1	3	3	3	20	25	22	10
2	1	2	3	5	0	13	10
2	2	3	1	44	29	37	42
2	3	1	2	30	27	30	21
3	1	3	2	20	15	17	25
3	2	1	3	17	29	20	24
3	3	2	1	37	28	37	20

Notice that the Orthogonal array is much larger.

The first step is again to determine how much variation has occurred between all treatments. The total variation is still determined by adding the square of each observation.

$$\text{Total Variation} = \sum x_i^2 = 23,443$$

The next step is to determine the effect of the grand mean as in the two level experiment.

$$\text{The Grand Mean Sum of Squares} = \frac{\left[\sum x_i\right]^2}{n} = 20,022.25$$

Determining the effect of the factors for an experiment of this size is a bit different than for the two level. Each factor level observation will be summed individually, squared and then divided by the number of observations at each level. The grand mean will then be subtracted.

$$\text{Effect Of The Factors} = S_T = \frac{T_1^2 + T_2^2 + T_3^2}{n} - \text{Grand Mean Sum of Squares}$$

T_1 for this problem is 272 and is determined by adding all observations for T at level one as highlighted below.

T	H	S	W	Observations			
1	1	1	1	15	27	22	17
1	2	2	2	30	21	36	27
1	3	3	3	20	25	22	10
2	1	2	3	5	0	13	10
2	2	3	1	44	29	37	42
2	3	1	2	30	27	30	21
3	1	3	2	20	15	17	25
3	2	1	3	17	29	20	24
3	3	2	1	37	28	37	20

T_2 is 288 and is determined by adding all of the level two observations for T.

$$S_T = \frac{272^2 + 288^2 + 289^2}{12} - 20,022.25$$

$$S_T = \frac{73,984 + 82,944 + 83,521}{12} - 20,022.25 = \mathbf{15.16}$$

This process is repeated for each factor and level.

$$S_H = \frac{186^2 + 356^2 + 307^2}{12} - 20,022.25 = \mathbf{1276.16}$$

$$S_S = \frac{279^2 + 264^2 + 306^2}{12} - 20,022.25 = \mathbf{75.5}$$

$$S_W = \frac{355^2 + 299^2 + 195^2}{12} - 20022.25 = \mathbf{1098.66}$$

The repetitional error effect can be determined in the same manner as earlier. The formula for finding the repetitional error effect for the experiment is

$$S_{e2} = S_T - S_m - \left[S_T + S_H + S_S + S_W \right]$$

The repetitional error effect is

$$S_{e2} = 23,443 - 20,022.3 - \left[15.2 + 1276.2 + 75.5 + 1098.6 \right]$$

$$= \mathbf{955.2}$$

DETERMINING THE SIGNIFICANCE OF THE FACTORS

The analysis of variance (ANOVA) table is used to organize the analysis of variation which occurs during the designed experiment and to attribute it to its source. Figure 12.6 is an ANOVA table for the experiment just completed.

The left hand column indicates the source of the variance. The df column indicates the number of degrees of freedom assigned to each source. The degree of freedom for the mean is one. The degree of freedom for each factor is the number of levels, which in this case is three, minus one. The degrees of freedom for

Source	df	S	V	F-Value
m	1	20,022.3	20,022.3	
T	2	15.2	7.6	.21
H	2	1,276.2	638.1	18.04
S	2	75.5	37.75	1.07
W	2	1,098.6	549.3	15.53
e 2	27	955.2	35.38	
Total	36	23,443.0		

Figure 12.6 ANOVA table.

the repetitional error effect (twenty-seven) is equal to the total number of obser-vations (thirty-six) minus the degrees of freedom assigned to all factors (eight) and the grand mean effect (one). The S column represents the sums of squares and is the amount of variation found at each stage of the experiment including the total variation, the grand mean, each of the factors and the repetitional error effect. The V column represents the average factor and error variance and is equal to the S column divided by the df column within source. The F-Value is determined by dividing each factor variance under the V column by the value of the repetitional error effect, also found under the V column. To determine whether a factor has significance the F-Values are compared to the critical value found in the F-Value table from Appendix A.2. The df for each factor (2) is located by moving across the top of the chart and the repetitional error (27) is located on the left side. The critical F-Value is located at the intersection of the two. The critical value is 3.35. Any F-Value for the experiment which equals or exceeds 3.35 is considered sig-nificant. The significant factors for the experiment are wave height and wave shape.

ADDITIONAL CONSIDERATIONS

Additional considerations in performing the design of experiment include the in-teractions between factor levels and noise factors. Interactions can occur between factors and in order to maximize the overall effectiveness of the experiment one factor level must be used in the presence of another. In the last experiment it was discovered that wave height and shape were significant. However, a specific wave height may be required for a specific wave shape in order to gain the largest reduction in overall bridging. A test for interaction must be conducted.

Certain factors cannot be controlled such as the weather but, may have an impact on the success of the experiment. An attempt must be made to predict optimal factor levels under different conditions or noise levels occurring which are not a controlled part of the experiment. The impact of noise must be determined.

DESIGNING THE EXPERIMENT TO INCREASE PROFIT

As stated earlier, the objective of the DOE process is to understand the impact of specific changes to the inputs of a process and then to maximize, minimize or nominalize the outcome by manipulating the input. From a global perspective, it should be clear at this point that an improvement made at a local level may have no impact or even a negative impact on profitability. The typical experiment designed to improve a quality characteristic at a specific resource may cause an increase in Operating Expense without creating an increase in Throughput. Experiments should be designed with this issue in mind.

• • •

During the initial design phase a determination should be made concerning the objective of the experiment and should include whether the objective is to support the attainment of the necessary condition or is to support the five step improvement process or both.

• • •

As in SPC, DOE must be studied based on how resources interface and the resulting global impact on the system. The product flow diagram and buffer management system will help tremendously in identifying what needs to be improved and handling the resulting impact.

In addition, consideration should be given to the impact a change in factor levels will have on other quality characteristics not found in the experiment and their impact on the ability to properly accomplish exploitation or subordination. In the wave solder experiment seen earlier, while temperature was not a factor in reducing bridging, it could have resulted in board warpage and major problems at other resources.

Consideration must also be given to the measurements desired in the outcome of the experiment. The nominalization of an outcome of an experiment may result in an equal amount of scrap or rework at a resource which appears between the constraint and the sales order and is loaded to 60%. The best alternative may not be the nominalization of the measurement if it results in an equal amount of scrap as well as rework. As seen in chapter eleven, for this portion of the net, a scrap will have far more impact than a rework.

PREDICTING THE IMPACT

Once the predicted outcome of the experiment has been determined another prediction must be made for the impact of the experiment on Throughput, Inventory
and Operating Expense. Determining the impact on Throughput from an overall
reduction of processing time on the constraint can be made by understanding how
a release of constraint time is to be used to create additional Throughput (see
chapter nine on exploiting the constraint). This is best accomplished by looking
at the overall schedule for the constraint. Key issues to consider include whether
or not the experimental design was product specific or whether it applied to all
products created on the constraint. Remember, that by changing constraint processing time the Throughput per unit of the constraint also changes and may result in
a change in the preferred product mix.

As stated earlier, determining the impact on Inventory and Operating Expense
may only be determined after an attempt has been made to subordinate to the
schedule created for the constraint in consideration of the predicted outcome of the
change in factor levels (see chapter three). Once a change has been made which
increases constraint availability there will be an immediate impact on those resources which must react to the increase but are themselves restricted in capacity.

SUPPORTING SPC

DOE is also used to support the SPC program. When an out of control condition
has been identified using SPC at a resource which is causing a threat to exploitation or subordination, DOE can be used to improve at that resource and bring the
process back into control or increase the Cpk by manipulating the input to either
maximize, minimize or nominalize the output.

PROBLEMS IN THE TAGUCHI LOSS FUNCTION

Developed by Genichi Taguchi, the Taguchi Loss Function equation is generally used to estimate the amount of loss associated with a specific measurement
within a process. The amount of loss is estimated for a specific measurement and
a baseline established which is then used to estimate all other losses associated with
individual measurements for the same process. The loss is computed using L =
$k(y - T)^2$ where k is a monetary constant, y is a response value and T is the target value.

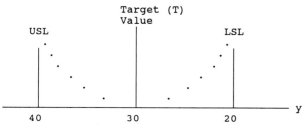

The value of k is determined by the following:

$$k = \frac{\text{Estimated Loss For y}}{(y - T)^2}$$

If the estimated loss for y = 20 equaled \$50 then

$$k = \frac{\$50}{(20 - 30)^2}$$

$$k = \frac{\$50}{100} = .5$$

The estimated loss for any measurement of y would be

$$L = .5 \ (y - T)^2$$

If y = 25 for the above then

$$L = .5 \ (25 - 30)^2$$

$$L = .5 \ x \ 25 = \$12.50$$

The Taguchi loss function assumes that k will be consistent for all measurements of y and that the closer to the target value the lower the loss. This is an isolated view of what is happening and, in fact, there are many more issues to consider. Whether or not a monetary loss actually occurs depends on what resource is being considered, what its position is within the plant, the degree of resource load and what type of loss is being considered. The assumption that k will be consistent for all measurements of y ignores the issue that on one side of the target value may be scrap and on the other may be rework. It also ignores the fact that one resource will have an impact on the measurements and monetary loss created at another resource. No one would argue that the further away from the target value, the more problems will occur. However, the degree of monetary impact is a different issue. The question which must be raised is, what is the impact on Throughput, Inventory and Operating Expense for any given measurement of y. As seen in chapter eleven on implementing SPC, the impact on Throughput at the constraint depends on the amount of constraint time absorbed by the scrap or rework and the rate at which the scrap or rework occurs. The farther away from the target value the more constraint time is absorbed due to replacing the scrapped part or accomplishing the rework. The impact on the non-constraint may or may not have any monetary impact at all. To understand what is important as in SPC a method must be used to determine the relationships between resources so that global issues can be addressed. To do this the product flow diagram is used. Figure 12.7 illustrates.

Resource R-6 exists between the constraint and the sales order. Any given measurement of y can have a different impact on Throughput. If a given measurement of y were to cause a scrap then the loss would be the total value of the sales order because the constraint must be used to replace the part. Therefore Throughput would decline. If a given measurement of y were to cause a rework R-6 has additional capacity to accomplish the rework. Throughput would not decline. However, what would be the impact if, at a certain measurement of y, R-6, due to the increased rework, would become constrained? If the constraint were large enough and surpassed the load on resource R-1 it would reduce the Throughput for the entire Throughput channel to whatever rate R-6 established. In figure 12.7, R-6's load has been increased to 120% due rework.

```
                          60%   Rework Load
                          60%   Normal Load
100%                     120%   Total  Load
    *-----*-----*-----*
  R-1    R-4   R-5   R-6
```

If R-6 were to have a rework load of 30% and not 60% the impact would be a bit different.

```
                          30%   Rework Load
                          60%   Normal Load
100%                      90%   Total  Load
    *-----*-----*-----*
  R-1    R-4   R-5   R-6
```

While R-6's load does not exceed R-1, it will probably cause delays in shipment and an increase in inventory in front of resource R-6. Throughput would decline slightly due to the late orders or operating expense would go up due to an increase in overtime to prevent late orders.

The measurement of one resource may have a direct relation to other resources within the net. Notice that R-3 has a direct relationship to R-1 through part operation 126/10. A given measurement of y causing a rework at 126/10 where excess and protective capacity would offset the impact could have a very negative

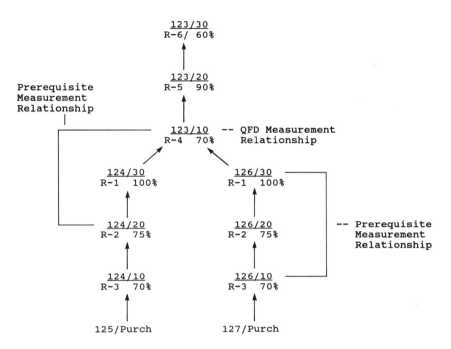

Figure 12.7 Product flow diagram.

effect on 126/30 where any loss of time will cause an immediate impact on throughput.

So, to understand the global impact of a specific measurement of y means that the following be known:

- The location within the product flow diagram of the resource on which y occurred.
- The location of the primary constraint.
- An estimate of the volume of scrap or rework which will occur as a result of the measurement.
- An estimate of the impact the additional resource load generated by the scrap or rework will have on non-constraining resources.
- The per part cost of raw material involved, if scrapped.
- The per product amount of sales involved.
- An estimate of the impact of the measurement on other resources (prerequisite measurements).

Before any estimate of loss can be determined an analysis of the physical environment must be made.

ADDITIONAL CONSIDERATIONS

Additional considerations include the loss to society and the loss due to additional wear by not producing products at the center of the specification. There is no argument against insuring that products are made as close to the center of the specification as possible. However, a monetary loss cannot be determined from the Taguchi Loss Function. It is a local measurement which cannot be used to judge the global impact with any certainty. It may result in misplaced priorities. From a local perspective a resource may have a larger "cost" due to rework but from a global perspective the loss may not exist. The magnitude of a problem is not the only factor to be considered.

OTHER DOE TECHNIQUES

The author used the Taguchi method in introducing the DOE concept because it seems to be the easiest to explain and for others to grasp. It should be understood that other techniques exist as well. Each seem to have good and bad points about them. However, each one must also be subject to the laws governing the dependent variable environment the same way in which the all the statistical methods used in this text are. For further study into DOE or other statistical methods the following texts are suggested:

Kiemele, Mark J. and Schmidt, Stephen R., Basic Statistics: Tools for Continuous Improvement, Air Academy Press, Colorado Springs, CO (1991).
Ryan, Thomas P., Statistical Methods for Quality Improvement, John Wiley and Sons, NY (1989).
Doty, Leonard A., Statistical Process Control, Industrial Press, NY (1991).

13

TQM II Implementation

This chapter will explore the process by which TQM II can and should be implemented.

OBJECTIVES

- To establish the basic sequence of events and to insure success.
- To create an understanding of what activities must be performed and why.
- To create an understanding of what to avoid during the process.

THE IMPLEMENTATION OVERVIEW

It is important to grasp the scope of the TQM II implementation program. The following is a list of issues which should be addressed and have been discussed to some extent. While these issues are not necessarily in the exact order of accomplishment they do show a basic flow.

- Establish the organization structure and re-write the corporate policy book. (Note: Re-writing the policy book to the TQM II world will require a paradigm shift in thinking, best accomplished through the education process).
- Develop the action plan for implementation of the five steps through utilization of the effect-cause effect process identifying what to change, what to change to, and how to cause change.
- Establish TQM II financial systems and begin collecting data and making decisions based on Throughput, Inventory, and Operating Expense.
- Analyze the dependent variable environment by developing product flow diagrams.

- Establish the QFD process by determining the definition for the necessary condition of good quality and extending it to the production process.
- Identify critical resources and develop the shop floor layout.
- Establish the DBR Process and begin buffer management.
- Identify and implement appropriate feedback mechanisms where necessary.
- Establish the supplier certification program.
- Document the process by creating the quality assurance, functional procedures and specifications manuals.
- Begin productivity focus. Plan location of constraints and methods of subordination.
- Begin the strategic planning process—Recession proof the company.
- Establish a permanent education program to support the requirements established under QFD and to maintain the TQM II improvement process.

BUILDING THE ORGANIZATIONAL STRUCTURE AND RE-WRITING THE POLICY BOOK

The first step in building the organizational structure and re-writing the policy book is to first begin the process of education. There must be a shift in thinking for those who are involved. Unless this shift takes place the new organizational structure will be in name only. People, regardless of level, will not do what they do not believe in. People must begin the process of leaving the cost world behind completely by re-writing their informal policy book. Once accomplished, the organization can be built, the formal policy book re-written and the development of the action plan begun.

It is the TQM II Executive and Quality Management councils who determine what the TQM II organizational structure is to be, guided by whether or not a program of continuous product improvement is to be endorsed and by what amount of support will be required to implement the action plan. While the functional organizations of marketing, production, purchasing, etc. will remain the same the focusing mechanisms and responsibilities will be modified.

BUILDING THE ACTION PLAN FOR IMPROVING PROFITS

Each company is different with regard to their physical environment and policies. This means that each company will also require different activities in order to improve. While there are certain aspects of each process to be implemented which will be similar in nature, the overall scope, tasks, sequencing of tasks, responsibilities, and the distribution of information will be different for each company. To develop an action plan which is effective for a specific company, the prerequisites for success should be known. From this list of prerequisites an action plan is developed. The action plan represents the implementation plan.

The prerequisite tree is created after a determination has been made to make a specific change in policy or the method of exploitation and subordination of the constraint has been selected. This means that a basic prerequisite to creating the action plan is to have completed the effect-cause-effect, assumption modeling and positive as well as prerequisite tree functions. The sequence of events in developing the implementation plan are:

Physical Constraint

*   Identify the limiting resource.
*   Determine how to get the maximum amount of Throughput from it.
*   Determine what all other resources must do to protect the "maximum amount of Throughput" being generated.
*   Determine what skill sets are required and who must be motivated.
*   Develop the action plan.

Policy Constraint

*   Identify what policy constraint needs to be changed (Effect-Cause-Effect).
*   Identify what new policy to adopt (Assumption Model).
*   Determine the impact of the change (Positive Trees).
*   Determine the prerequisites to change (Prerequisite Tree).
*   List the actions necessary to accomplish the prerequisites (Action Plan).

(Note: Physical constraints can be identified through the use of either Effect-Cause-Effect or through diagnostic software. However, diagnostic software is capable of generating tremendous insight as to the relationship of all resources and the impact of the change before it is made in the physical world).

ESTABLISHING THE PERMANENT EDUCATION PROGRAM

Obviously, statistical process control and design of experiments are necessary skills needed by shop people and engineering to gain and maintain control over specific processes. However, to accomplish the kind of paradigm shift which is being advocated in this book will require a different type of motivation. There are two issues which must be overcome, fear and the "not invented here" syndrome. Change causes fear which gives rise to resistance. This resistance can paralyze any attempt at a successful implementation, specifically if excess capacity is seen as a problem and not a weapon. The not invented here syndrome can be just as disastrous. Whenever one portion of the organization has been successful at breaking the constraint and it moves to another function there will be a certain amount of resistance from those people in the function in which the new constraint now resides. This situation is made worse when those people who have just broken the constraint are now trying to get the people in the new constraint area to implement the five step process. To reduce the impact of these two issues the concept of encouraging people to invent their own solutions is used. The inventor of a specific concept will have very little fear of change and a total lack of "not invented here" resistance. This kind of "realization training" can be accomplished by simulation. Placing the student in an environment where a decision must be made and then seeing what the impact of that decision is, will have a long lasting effect. Simulations are more adaptable to "real life" situations than simply reading a book. However, the likelihood that a simulation can be created for all situations is nil and it is not always desirable to rely on a simulation to motivate people. What is needed on the part of the motivator is an ability to create, within the people to be motivated, a thorough understanding of the cause and effect relationships as well as the assumptions involved in the problem. Being a group facilitator and leading people through the effect-cause-effect, evaporating clouds and positive trees process will allow people to create, for themselves, simple solutions for which they are responsible and not the facilitator. Obviously, the facilitator must know something about the process and must have worked through the problem himself prior to leading the group. The best group facilitator will be the manager responsible for the group he is leading. Managers should be trained to perform the function of the group facilitator.

Sometimes group facilitation is not always desirable. In this case the manager must know just the right question to ask to unlock the intuition of the person he is trying to motivate. As an example, in chapter five quality cost was approached by presenting a specific situation and then asking what the impact would be under obvious conditions—thus making quality cost a questionable focusing mechanism in the mind of the reader. This approach required no real education process. It did require that a thorough study of the effect-cause effect process regarding quality cost issues be made.

A balanced education program will incorporate a number of different methodologies to help motivate and to transfer technical know-how including books, workbooks, classroom instruction, simulations and facilitation. However, unlike past education programs which concentrate on a shotgun approach to education. A focused approach should be taken to understand who needs to know what and when they need to know it. The education implementation plan should be incorporated in the overall implementation plan which is defined by the list of prerequisites assigned to the goal. As an example, the constraint has been identified as a lathe in the production facility. What are the prerequisites to exploitation and subordination? What must occur to maximize the amount of money currently being made from the constraint and what must happen to subordinate the rest of the resources to the way in which it has been decided to exploit the lathe? To maximize what Throughput can be created by the constraint, no parts should be made by the constraint which are defective, a valid schedule must be created and followed, defective parts should not reach the constraint, engineering should minimize what time is used by the constraint to make parts and, the product mix should also be set to maximize Throughput. What actions will be required to see that each person is able to fulfill their requirement? Each person must not be blocked by thinking in an illogical manner with respect to exploitation. Each person must also understand how to exploit. Is the quality engineer capable of establishing a capability index for the constraint and implementing an effective statistical process control monitoring system? Can production be convinced not to deviate from the schedule? Can engineering implement a properly focused setup reduction program? When these questions are answered then an implementation plan can be created.

If education is to be used to motivate and to have people invent their own solutions on a day to day basis it must be a permanently integral part of the overall program and be available on a regular basis. In addition, the ability to simulate the actual environment will result in a tremendous amount of knowledge being transferred. The amount of investigative work that can be accomplished through diagnostic simulations is irreplaceable and should be considered part of the overall learning process.

ANALYSIS OF THE CURRENT ENVIRONMENT

Understanding the way in which resources interface so that the proper actions can take place is the subject of the product flow analysis, and is one of the first activities performed in an attempt to understand the company. Product flow diagrams are created which document each step in the way products flow through the facility. See chapter three.

THE SURVEY

It is important to have the knowledge of where each function within the organization is with regard to their acceptance and understanding of the tasks to be performed and what the requirements are from two perspectives; to understand what must be changed and to determine how the change will occur. Most change will occur after a person understands that a need to change exists and that they feel that they have the ability to make the change occur. The survey is designed so that a manager can understand what skill sets and procedures are lacking so that a plan of action can be made to correct it. However, there are other perspectives which must be considered. As mentioned earlier, a survey tends to look at the magnitude of a problem without consideration for actual problems connected to the five step process and may tend to cloud the issue by diluting the overall effort. Before the survey is performed it must be understood that it should be conducted after the constraint has been identified and a determination has been made of how to exploit and subordinate. The issue to be determined is whether or not the proper skill sets are available to successfully accomplish the exploitation and subordination phase?

ESTABLISHING EMPLOYEE INVOLVEMENT TEAMS AND QC CIRCLES

The first step in the development of an employee-involved TQM II program is to establish the concept of a valid focusing mechanism through education. The next step is to reinforce the first by changing the employee's environment, the method by which feedback is received and the way individual work goals are established:

- Establish the Employee Involvement and QC Circles team concept through education in TQM II concepts and elementary tools including; statistical process control, Pareto analysis, effect-cause-effect, assumption modeling, positive trees, prerequisite trees and action planning as well as DBR concepts, buffer management and brain storming.
- Clear and simplify the work environment; have a place for everything and keep the work area cleared of any tool or product that is not currently being used.
- Establish rules for resource activation and determining priorities and insure that priorities are easily determined.
- Establish feedback mechanisms including source inspections (next process and poka yoke) and the buffer management process where necessary to support the exploitation and subordination processes.
- Begin regular meetings to improve communication, reenforce the TQM II concepts and determine what actions must be taken to exploit the constraint and to subordinate the remaining resources.
- Document the process.

IMPLEMENTING DRUM-BUFFER-ROPE

The DBR implementation process begins with education. Specific educational requirements include:

- How resources interface.
- How a schedule should be generated.
- What the rules of resource activation are.
- How material releases are determined.
- What the five step process of "continuous profit improvement" are.
- How to exploit the constraint.
- How to properly subordinate.
- How to make decisions.

The next step is to analyze and establish relationships between resources to build an understanding of the overriding characteristics of the manufacturing facility. The key issue being whether the problems encountered are characteristic of an A-plant, T-plant, V-plant or a combination of each.

Once the plant type has been determined and the constraints have been located, rules for resource activation and determining priorities can be set. Shop documentation will be required for maintaining order identity and continuity. While the traditional work order is no longer needed for dispatching and determining priorities or to support cost accounting, the traditional MRP II work order system will generate shop paper for material kitting and routing and support the reporting of material movement through the shop.

Additional documentation includes:

- A schedule for all constraint resources.
- A schedule for resources which appear immediately after a diverging operation to prevent stealing of material.
- A raw material release schedule to coordinate the release of material with the constraint schedule.
- A raw material requirements report to notify purchasing of the quantity and need date.
- A sales order due date report to keep track of customer commitments.
- A buffer management report to execute the buffer. management process.

While documentation is being generated the shop floor layout can be rearranged insuring ample spacing for buffer inventories and reducing the amount of space for non-constraint resource inventories.

Once the shop paper has been completed a schedule for the constraint should be generated to set priorities for production and to determine the requirements of all other resources through the development of the rope (see chapter six). An estimate of the amount of aggregated protection necessary in front of the various buffer origins including the shipping, constraint and assembly operations will be needed to determine the release dates for raw material. Buffer sizes should be oversized estimates until some indication of the performance of buffer zones is available. As more information is obtained about the make-up of each zone cross section the size of the buffer can be increased or decreased as necessary. (See chapter six on buffer management).

Most manufacturing facilities will be starting with excess material in work in process (WIP). This material can be downsized through attrition, insuring that it is not replaced or it can be completely withdrawn from the production floor. Obviously, obsolete material should be totally withdrawn. Production batch sizes should be determined by the sales order or finished goods forecast. The planning of overlapping operations can be accomplished by first determining what the size of the transfer batch should be and then begin moving material by the transfer batch size. Remember, the smaller the transfer batch the shorter the lead time will be.

It may be convenient but not necessarily required to co-locate resources into cells which use the same part/operations repetitively so that transfer batch sizes can be held to a minimum. Remember, however, that improvements should be made so that profit goes up. Cells do not guarantee that profits will go up, nor does a transfer batch size of one.

A Cell is a close assemblage of operations which cuts down on distance traveled and the support necessary to move material. In one form of cell, the U-line, the operator(s) stands in the middle of the "U" and may operate more than one machine as illustrated by the following.

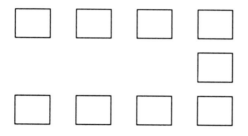

At this time the constraint schedule can be generated and the material release schedule created along with the buffer management reports so that production can begin. Be sure to document the production process and the rules of resource activation and improvement so that workers can have a ready reference.

CREATING THE TQM II FINANCIAL SYSTEM

The TQM II financial system is simple and very straight forward. What needs to be understood is what the past, current as well as predicted Throughput, Inventory and Operating Expense figures will be. Total Throughput is equal to Total sales minus the total cost of raw material. Since incremental cost buildups are unable to reflect the true value of any product the labor and overhead figures for assemblies, sub-assemblies and finished products can be eliminated. The cost of goods sold figure for most accounting systems would then reflect raw material only. Most systems also reflect sales price. The profit margin figure which is equal to the sales price minus cost of goods sold would then represent Throughput whether looking at past history, current status or forecast. This may cause a problem with the tax man or with corporate offices who have very definite opinions as to how inventories should be valued. There may be a requirement to keep two sets of books. One for the audit and one for making decisions and understanding the true health of the company.

Inventories will include the value of raw material contained in raw material, work in process and finished goods inventories. But, also includes the assets of the corporation which cannot be easily withdrawn such as machines, buildings, desks and computers. Operating expenses include the day to day expenses for any type of labor, insurance, office supplies, taxes and utilities. A separate report can be generated along with separate major accounts for all three account types in most accounting software packages and current accounts grouped under major accounts for Throughput, Inventory and Operating Expense.

GETTING STARTED

In the process of trying to determine what to fix and to develop the implementation plan it is sometimes difficult to know where to start. It is important not to lose sight of the objective and that is to increase profitability by implementing the five step improvement process. The first step is to identify the constraint. In accomplishing this first step it is often usefull to try to isolate the constraint by function. Some sample questions to propose might be:

"If you had to deliver 20% more product from manufacturing could you do it"?

If not,

"Would you have to obtain more resources from outside the company"?

This will determine whether the constraint is inside the company or outside in the market. If the constraint is in the market and the answer is "yes, we could deliver", then ask

"Why aren't you selling more?"

and begin to assemble the effect-cause-effect diagram and look for the core cause. Or, ask

"How can we get more out of the market?"

and begin the exploitation process. If the constraint is internal to the company and the answer is no, we cannot deliver, ask

"Why can't we deliver more?"

If a physical resource is found to be acting as if it were the constraint try to determine how to exploit it. Build a schedule for it. Try to maximize its availability. It may be found during this process that the constraint is not physical but, due to the way in which the suspect resource is being managed, it is limiting the creation of Throughput.

After the constraint has been exploited determine what needs to be done by all the other resources to support the constraint. At this point it may be found that other resources are also restricted and because of a restriction elsewhere it may be difficult to exploit the constraint to its fullest. What may have been discovered is the secondary constraint. Begin to exploit the secondary constraint. In trying to squeeze the maximum out of the secondary constraint two things are occuring.

- The first is that the subordination of the secondary constraint to the primary constraint will be accomplished and secondly,
- Preparation will be made to manage the new constraint when the primary one is broken.

As an example, the market may be the constraint. But, because of a limit in production the manufacturing manager states that he cannot deliver 20% more product if it were sold. But, he could deliver 5%. In this case the market would be considered the primary constraint while production would be the secondary constraint. It is extremely important that, because the constraint is in the market, all orders be delivered on time. So, production must be subordinated to the market. That resource which is considered the secondary constraint should be exploited to insure that it can be subordinated to the market. So, a schedule should be created for the limiting resource, and an improvement program should be implemented to maximize its ability to deliver to the schedule created by the market. All other applicable resources should be subordinated to the secondary constraint.

What has happened at this time is that the secondary constraint and all other resources have been prepared for the day when the primary constraint is elevated.

While attempting to exploit the market it may be found that a basic concept such as cost is preventing the maximum amount of Throughput from being generated. Once market segmentation is accomplished and excess capacity is sold the constraint will immediately move inside the company. More than likely it will move to the secondary constraint. Remember, that once this occurs the marketing strategy must change to insure that the internal constraint is fully exploited. Then begin to understand what must be done to properly subordinate all resources to the new constraint.

It is very important not to be limited in creative thought. Addressing the improvement process by using the five steps will help tremendously on being able to focus the thought process and will promote creativeness.

14

Facing the Strategic Issues

This chapter addresses some key issues with respect to strategic planning and offers insights into how to grow and protect a company's ability to create profits.

OBJECTIVES

- To create an understanding of market segmentation strategy and its overall implementation.
- To create an understanding of how to grow a company and the importance of the utilization of resources in the creation of Throughput as well as in the support of the market segmentation strategy.
- To create an understanding of the concept of long term planning as it applies to the five step improvement process and the impact of new product introduction.
- To begin to understand how to recession proof a company.
- To understand the impact of the farmout strategy on profitability.
- To define the role of the diagnostic system.

MARKET SEGMENTATION

Possibly the most important and yet the least understood tool in strategic planning is the impact of an effective market segmentation program. Market segments are designed to maximize the use of resources in the production of Throughput and to minimize the risk of a downturn. There are three rules in market segmentation. Market segments should be selected so that:

- The sales price in one market will not impact the sales price in another.
- The same resource base is serving all markets.
- It is unlikely that all segments will be down at the same time.

215

The benefit to an effective program is the ability to protect valuable resources and to maximize profitability by manipulating the market to fit capacity instead of manipulating capacity to fit market demand. By manipulating the sales price for products which are made on non-constraint resources, it is possible to increase product demand and thereby increase demand for time on those resources which are being under utilized. Since the real profit for these products is the difference between the sales price and the cost of raw material, a large amount of profit can still be generated during those times when there is a downturn of demand on some resources.

There are many ways to segment the market; geographical, product, time, customer type, the list is very large. Probably one of the more effective is product segmentation where two products are similar but, with minor changes can serve different markets and demand different prices. Even when product configurations are more complex, it may be more profitable to sell them at a lower price to a different market if the additional products are produced on resources which have excess capacity. A good example of this is in the computer industry where a basic product is sold at one price and the same product with minor add-ons is sold at a lower price into the same customer base.

Geographic market segmentation involves the sale of products into two different geographical locations. The product can be the same exact part, but because of a geographical difference is sold at a lower price to fill excess capacity.

A market segmentation based on time may take advantage of a lead time which is shorter than the industry average by segmenting prices to lead times. The average lead time may be one week for a company to produce a circuit board for its customers, while the industry average may be six weeks. The company may set its prices based on the industry average lead time of six weeks. If the customer wants it in two weeks it will pay a premium. While it does not cost the board manufacturer any more money to produce the board, the company can manipulate the price for earlier delivery to protect its resources.

But, product pricing is not be the only issue which can be manipulated through market segmentation. In those segmented markets into which excess capacity is being sold, what would be the impact to product acceptance if the additional profit being generated were used to increase the quality or functionality of the products being produced? The following figure is used to illustrate.

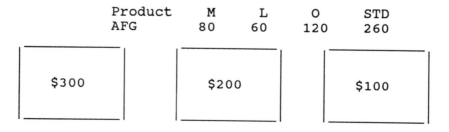

Product AFG	M	L	O	STD
	80	60	120	260
	$300		$200	$100

In the $200 market, while selling excess capacity, the profit will be the difference between the $200 sales price and the $80 raw material price. What would be the impact to product acceptance in the $200 market if $20 of additional raw material were to be added making the total raw material investment $100? Or, if 5–10 hours of additional labor was used to enhance the product. If done with excess capacity, the profit is still $200 minus the $100 cost of raw material. This strategy would be a way of increasing product quality, decreasing the sales price and gaining market share? It provides a tremendous competitive advantage.

GROWING THE COMPANY

Obviously a company can grow by implementing the five step improvement process, but at what point does it know when to add employees, buy new resources or build new plants? New plants are added when there is no capacity left in the old plant. When everything is done to squeeze as much Throughput as possible from the old plant and all resources are being fully utilized, not just activated, only then should consideration be given to buying a new plant. The question should be asked at this point whether the resources in the new plant can be protected through adequate market segmentation. If the answer is no, then an effort must be made to look for new segments to support the building of the plant. When this question can be answered satisfactorily then the plant can be built.

Adding employees should be done with the idea in mind that they are a permanent fixture. Whenever employees are added it is the responsibility of management to do everything within their power to keep them. Employees are added so that Throughput can be protected or additional Throughput generated as part of the five step process. They are kept by insuring that resources are fully utilized in the creation of Throughput. If employees are led to believe that their efforts to increase the amount of excess capacity available through the improvement process will not be used to protect but to threaten their jobs, the improvement process will then become threatened. In addition, whenever employees are laid off they end up eventually getting jobs in companies where their expertise and experience levels are most in line with the job requirements. Those jobs will be at competitive companies. When a major personal computer manufacturer which had broken all records in growth during its first few years in business was having financial difficulty for the first time, it fired it's president and laid off an estimated 1,000–1,400 people. Within a week a major competitor had ads in the local newspaper wanting to hire them. What better way to pick up good people trained by one of the best computer manufacturers in the world.

Much like employees, machines are added when it is necessary in the implementation of the five step process. Obviously, if a machine becomes the constraint and it is elevated, Throughput should go up. However, there are a number of conditions where the best option is to maintain the constraint in its current location. Whenever a constraint is elevated and it moves to a machine which is processing parts irradically, due to poor quality or increased down time, the production process becomes unpredictable. Constraint resources which feed themselves in the process will cause Inventory to begin climbing and increase the amount of unpredictability. Before a machine is purchased to elevate the constraint, the location of the new constraint should be known and its impact predicted.

It may also be necessary to buy a machine so that the subordination process can be accomplished. If a resource is a secondary constraint and is loaded to 90% capacity, it may be impossible to subordinate it to the primary constraint. In this case a resource is elevated to smooth out the scheduling process and maintain predictability.

Companies can grow without adding resources by growing into the strong links within the chain. This is the objective of a market segmentation program.

LONG TERM PLANNING

Whether its long or short term planning, the objective is to live and profit by the limitations provided. Long term planning can involve breaking the current constraint, specific market constraints may take a long period of time to be elevated, or in manipulating and predicting where the constraint will appear next. If the constraint is a specific machine within production and it is supporting a certain level of profitability, what will be the impact of breaking the constraint? Where will it appear next and what actions will be required? If it goes into the market, how should the five step improvement process be implemented? To simply wait until the last constraint is elevated and then find out where it went is like playing Russian roulette. In some instances the identification process should simply be a verification that the constraint is where it was predicted to be.

NEW PRODUCT INTRODUCTION

Whenever new products are introduced into a company there is a certain amount of disruption for those resources which are controlling the generation of Throughput. New products which take time from the constraint will also take Throughput. Managers should be aware that unless the Throughput generated per unit of the constraint is equal to or higher than current production, Throughput will go down. The impact of new products can be minimized during the design process by planning the use of non-constrained resources for production. This will allow the company the ability to maintain a certain price advantage during the introduction period and also an ability to generate higher levels of Throughput during a critical period when the expenses for new product development and market introduction are high. Disruptions in the schedule will be nonexistent since non-constraint resources will still be able to produce to the schedule presented by the constraint. Since this is also a period of uncertainty for the new product, risk is held to a minimum. The cost of production is the price of raw material, and even a certain amount of that can be recovered. In situations where it is impossible to not use a specific resource and that resource is the constraint, new products should minimize its use. An alternative would be to move the constraint to a new location where the Throughput generated would be higher and the restrictions to the new product would be less.

In many cases the introduction of new products will increase the load on non-constraint resources to the extent that the probability is low that they will be able to deliver to the constraint on time, requiring that buffer sizes be increased or that overtime be required to maintain current schedules. This means that while Throughput has not suffered, Inventory and Operating Expenses have gone up. This should be considered in the expense of introducing a new product.

RECESSION PROOFING THE COMPANY

Companies move into stagnation and decline when they fail to implement the five step improvement process, for whatever reason. In a recessional period the ability to continue this process seems more difficult due to the shrinking market size. Dealing with issues of marketing constraints is not something most companies are comfortable with. However, it does not mean that it becomes impossible.

Recession proofing a company means that regardless of the economic status of the environment in which a company exists it should be able to continue growing. There are three major issues:

- The ability to continuously implement the five step improvement process.
- The ability to minimize the impact of a recession by protecting resources.
- A valid decision process.

It is imperative that companies understand how to consistently identify, exploit, subordinate, elevate and repeat the process regardless of the situation. The better a management group is at this process, the more isolated from threat they become.

Whenever companies enter a period of decline, there are two events which seem almost inevitable; the layoff and the re-organization. One occurs to satisfy the immediate concerns of the stockholders and that is to increase profitability by reducing cost. The other occurs to either consolidate operations so that costs can be further reduced or to segment resources in an attempt to increase control, thereby increasing future Throughput. However, as has been stated before, Operating Expense exists to support and protect the creation of Throughput. Before any measure is taken to reduce Operating Expense a determination as to the identity of the constraint as well as the method of exploitation and subordination must be made. Reducing Operating Expense before knowing what will be required to elevate the constraint is dangerous. In the section on decision making, product pricing was discussed. The importance of excess capacity in gaining a competitive advantage of pricing in a specific market segmentation should be clear. If the method of exploitation of the market is to find an isolated segment and dump excess capacity at a reduced price, reducing excess capacity will reduce the effectiveness of this alternative by reducing the amount of money that can be generated.

Segmenting resources in the face of a marketing constraint usually means that the same market must absorb more Operating Expense. In recession proofing a company, the objective is to have a large number of market segments being fed by the same resources thereby protecting those resources that are available. Resource segmentation or plant expansion should only occur when no excess capacity exists in the current plant and enough market segments exist so that even if one market falls others are there to absorb available resource capacity. If a marketing constraint and excess capacity exists at the same time, the rule is to find a market segment and dump products into that market for any amount you can get above the cost of raw material.

Without a valid decision process based on absolute measurements and an understanding of the relationships between resources, all the preparation in the world will not help to avoid the inevitable. Companies are doomed to react to the environment instead of molding it to fit their needs.

THE FARMOUT STRATEGY

There are many ways to commit corporate suicide but one of the most devastating and probably the most prevalent is the farm out strategy. Companies who are having a tough time competing and need a quick solution invariably begin comparison shopping between the cost of doing business in-house and the cost of buying parts and sub assemblies from vendors and assembling in-house. Unfortunately, the short term winners usually tend to be the vendors who supply the parts not the corporation who gave them the business. The corporation who farmed out the material begins to lose immediately, while, in the long run, everyone loses. As the company begins to farm out products the labor and overhead assigned to the parts now coming from the vendor must be distributed to the parts which are still being built in-house. The overhead distribution becomes larger and larger until it is obvious that no parts can be made in house which can compete with vendor prices. The following figure is a cost buildup for two similar parts made in house.

	Material Cost	Labor Cost	Overhead Cost	Standard Cost	Sales Price	Profit Margin
A	80	60	120	260	300	40
B	80	80	160	320	310	-10
					Net Profit	30

Under the cost matrix it looks as if part B is not profitable and a solution must be implemented which will bring costs down for B. A vendor is located which is ready to supply B for $200. Initially, the solution seems to work. However, unless the total overhead and labor force is reduced operating expense will not go down. The labor and overhead must now be placed solely on A.

	Material Cost	Labor Cost	Overhead Cost	Standard Cost	Sales Price	Profit Margin
A	80	140	280	500	300	-200
B	200				310	+110
					Net Profit	- 90

This may seem a trivial issue but, has resulted in the downfall of many corporations. The make/buy decision is considered in chapter five on correcting the decision process.

Whether a product should be farmed out should be made based on its impact to Throughput, Inventory an Operating Expense, not cost. And, the primary issue should be on Throughput.

THE ROLE OF THE DIAGNOSTICS SYSTEM

In small, medium and large companies, depending on the complexity and nature of the business, it may be desirable to use computer based diagnostic equipment as an analysis tool for environments where resources are dependent on each other and are subject to variation in their ability to produce. TQM diagnostic software is designed to react to the nuances of the dependent variable environment through simulation. It understands the relationships between resources and acts to simulate the impact of external effects on the current balance or lack of balance between resources. The objective is to present a platform for analyzing and focusing the improvement program under the total quality management umbrella. It should be capable of helping to answering questions such as what the impact of a certain setup reduction program might be at a specific resource on the other resources in the plant and, ultimately, return on investment.

In addition, it should also lend insight by showing the absence of a particular influence. As an example, excess capacity is an indication that a certain marketing constraint exists. The absence of demand on resources which have more than enough capacity to create additional product at the cost of raw material is an indication of a poor market segmentation policy. While this may not be the case, it should lead to a study of how to exploit the excess capacity and provide a road map for the development of new products or the sale of old ones.

Diagnostic equipment are vital in being able to:

*   Identify Physical constraints.
*   Identify Policy constraints.
*   Initiate Valid schedules.
*   Implement Improvement Programs.

APPLICATIONS

Engineering should be able to use TQM diagnostics equipment to support a wide variety of activities including total productive maintenance, set up reduction, statistical programs such as SPC, DOE and multi-vari analysis, design for manufacturability, and process improvements. Finance should be able to validate quickly any requests for capital equipment by Throughput justification.

Perhaps the most important application is the ability to use it in analyzing the strategic positioning of the company. It is an integral part of the recession proofing process. It helps in determining what products should be sold in what markets, what the economic impact is of buying an additional plant and how the company should grow to minimize the impact of a downturn in the economy.

CONSTRUCTION

The TQM diagnostic software should work by creating a valid schedule, since this is what ultimately determines the capabilities and limitations of the system. To do this it must understand the way in which resources interface and react accordingly. When the schedule is produced, demand is known for each resource, what the extent of excess and protective capacity is and what the relationships are between resources. Any change in the environment effecting the schedule will have a direct impact on Throughput, since Throughput is created by the delivery of the product. Inventory and Operating Expense exist to support the schedule and will be effected by either increasing or decreasing depending on the change in demand created by a change in the schedule. The result is a model of the impact on Throughput, Inventory and Operating Expense created by a change.

Bibliography

Doty, Leonard A., Statistical Process Control, Industrial Press, NY (1991).

Goldratt, Eliyahu, The Goal, North River Press, Croton-on-Hudson, NY (1984).

Hall, Robert W., Zero Inventories, Dow Jones Irwin, Homewood, IL (1983).

Hauser, John R. and Clausing, Don, The House of Quality, Harvard Business Review, Vol. 66, No. 3 (1988).

Imai, Masaki, Kaizen: The Key to Japan's Competitiveness, Random House, NY (1986).

Ishikawa, Kaoru, What is Quality Control? Prentice Hall, Inc., Englewood Cliffs, NJ (1985)

Japan Management Association, Kanban: Just in Time at Toyota, Productivity Press, Cambridge, MA (1986).

Juran, J. M., Juran's Quality Control Hand Book—Fourth Addition, McGraw-Hill, NY (1988).

Kaplan, Robert, Global Solutions Presentation (video). National Association of Accountants, Boston, May (1990).

Kiemele, Mark J. and Schmidt, Stephen R., Basic Statistics: Tools for Continuous Improvement, Air Academy Press, Colorado Springs, CO (1991).

King, Bob, Better Designs in Half the Time: Implementing (QFD) Quality Function Deployment in America, Goal/QPC, Meuthen, MA (1987).

Mizuno, Shigeru, Management for Quality Improvement: The 7 New Tools, Productivity Press, Cambridge, MA (1988).

Nakajima, Seiichi, Introduction to Total Productive Maintenance, Productivity Press, Cambridge, MA (1988).

Oakland, John S., Total Quality Management, Nichols Publishing, NY (1990).

Osburn, Moran, Musselwhite and Zenger, Self-Directed Work Teams: The New American Challenge, Business One Irwin, Homewood, IL (1990).

223

Ryan, Thomas P., Statistical Methods for Quality Improvement, John Wiley and Sons, NY (1989).

Scherkenbach, William W., Deming's Road to Continual Improvement, SPC Press, Knoxville, TN (1991).

Shingo, Shegeo, A Revolution in Manufacturing: The SMED System, Productivity Press, Cambridge, MA (1985).

Shingo, Shegeo, Zero Quality Control: Source Inspection and the Poka Yoke System, Productivity Press, Cambridge, MA (1986).

Stein, Robert E., Beyond Statistical Process Control, Production and Inventory Management Journal, Vol. 32, No. 1 (1991).

Suzaki, Kiyoshi, The New Manufacturing Challenge, Free Press, NY (1987).

Umble, Michael M. and Srikanth, M. L., Synchronous Manufacturing: Principles of World Class Excellence, Southwestern Publishing Co. Cincinatti, Ohio, (1990).

Appendix

Normal Table and F Table

Table A.1 Normal Table

Z		.00	.01	.02	.03	.04	.05	.06	.07	.08	.09
3.2	3	68714	66367	64095	61895	59765	57703	55706	53774	51904	50094
3.3		48342	46648	45009	43423	41889	40406	38971	37584	36243	34946
3.4		33693	32481	31311	30179	29086	28029	27009	26023	25071	24151
3.5		23263	22405	21577	20778	20006	19262	18543	17849	17180	16534
3.6		15911	15310	14730	14171	13632	13112	12611	12128	11662	11213
3.7		10780	10363	99611	95740	92010	88417	84957	81624	78414	75324
3.8	4	72348	69483	66726	64072	61517	59059	56694	54418	52228	50122
3.9		48096	46148	44274	42473	40741	39076	37475	35936	34458	33037
4.0		31671	30359	29099	27888	26726	25609	24536	23507	22518	21569
4.1		20657	19783	18944	18138	17365	16624	15912	15230	14575	13948
4.2		13346	12769	12215	11685	11176	10689	10221	97736	93447	89337
4.3	5	85399	81627	78015	74555	71241	68069	65031	62123	59340	56675
4.4		54125	51685	49350	47117	44979	42935	40980	39110	37322	35612
4.5		33977	32414	30920	29492	28127	26823	25577	24386	23249	22162
4.6		21125	20133	19187	18283	17420	16597	15810	15060	14344	13660
4.7		13008	12386	11792	11226	10686	10171	96796	92113	87648	83391
4.8	6	79333	75465	71779	68267	64920	61731	58693	55799	53043	50418

Table A.2 F Table

DF	1	2	3	4	5	6	7	8	9	10
1	161.44	199.50	215.69	224.57	230.16	233.98	236.78	238.89	240.55	241.89
2	18.51	19.00	19.16	19.25	19.30	19.33	19.35	19.37	19.39	19.40
3	10.13	9.55	9.28	9.12	9.01	8.94	8.89	8.85	8.81	8.79
4	7.71	6.94	6.59	6.39	6.26	6.16	6.09	6.04	6.00	5.96
5	6.61	5.79	5.41	5.19	5.05	4.95	4.88	4.82	4.77	4.74
6	5.99	5.14	4.76	4.53	4.39	4.28	4.21	4.15	4.10	4.06
7	5.59	4.74	4.35	4.12	3.97	3.87	3.79	3.73	3.68	3.64
8	5.32	4.46	4.07	3.84	3.69	3.58	3.50	3.44	3.39	3.35
9	5.12	4.26	3.86	3.63	3.48	3.37	3.29	3.23	3.18	3.14
10	4.96	4.10	3.71	3.48	3.33	3.22	3.14	3.07	3.02	2.98
11	4.84	3.98	3.59	3.36	3.20	3.09	3.01	2.95	2.90	2.85
12	4.75	3.89	3.49	3.26	3.11	3.00	2.91	2.85	2.80	2.75
13	4.67	3.81	3.41	3.18	3.03	2.92	2.83	2.77	2.71	2.67
14	4.60	3.74	3.34	3.11	2.96	2.85	2.76	2.70	2.65	2.60
15	4.54	3.68	3.29	3.06	2.90	2.79	2.71	2.64	2.59	2.54
16	4.69	6.63	3.24	3.01	2.85	2.74	2.66	2.59	2.54	2.49
17	4.45	3.59	3.20	2.96	2.81	2.70	2.61	2.55	2.49	2.45
27	4.21	3.35	2.96	2.73	2.57	2.46	2.37	2.31	2.25	2.20

Index